Anonymous

Cultus Arborum

A Descriptive Account of Phallic Tree Worship

Anonymous

Cultus Arborum

A Descriptive Account of Phallic Tree Worship

ISBN/EAN: 9783743385115

Manufactured in Europe, USA, Canada, Australia, Japa

Cover: Foto ©ninafisch / pixelio.de

Manufactured and distributed by brebook publishing software (www.brebook.com)

Anonymous

Cultus Arborum

CULTUS ARBORUM

A DESCRIPTIVE ACCOUNT OF

Phallic Tree Worship

WITH ILLUSTRATIVE

LEGENDS, SUPERSTITIONS, USAGES, &C.,

EXHIBITING ITS

ORIGIN AND DEVELOPMENT

AMONGST THE

Eastern & Western Nations of the World

FROM THE EARLIEST TO MODERN TIMES;

WITH A BIBLIOGRAPHY OF WORKS UPON AND REFERRING TO THE PHALLIC CULTUS.

PRIVATELY PRINTED.

1890.

PREFACE.

THE present volume forms a companion to three already issued on "Ancient and Modern Symbol Worship," denominated severally, "Phallism," "Ophiolatreia," "Phallic Objects and Remains," and "Tree Worship," they all form parts of one whole, and constitute a Series on the various forms and phases of what is known as "Phallic Worship."

The subject is an extensive one, and there still remain sections of it which have not yet been dealt with, but which may be exhibited in future volumes. Although in the compass of the present work it has been impossible to treat the subject in anything like an exhaustive manner, a great deal of matter has been incorporated in its closely-printed pages which, attentively perused, will enable the reader to form a just opinion of what is included in the title.

At the end of this volume we have endeavoured to give the student of Ancient Faiths a Bibliography of works on or connected with Phallism.

Being the first attempt of the kind, omissions will doubtless be found, although there are nearly five hundred references given, yet even as it is, it will prove of great use and advantage to those making researches. It is divided into two classes—Phallic works, and books bearing more or less upon the subject.

CONTENTS.

                                                                                      PAGE.

CHAPTER I. 1

    Characteristics of Trees—Naturalness of Tree Worship—Origin of the worship—The Tree of Life—Ancient Types—A Tree as a Symbol of Life—Poetical Associations—Sacred Fig-tree—India specially a land of Tree Worship—Trees identified with Gods—Meritoriousness of planting Trees—Auspicious and inauspicious Trees—Ceremonies connected with Tree Worship—Invocation of Tree Gods—Banian Tree—Ritual directions—Santal Worship.

CHAPTER II. 16

    The Bael-tree—Worship of the Left Hand—Trees of the Sun and Moon—The Arbre Sec, or Dry Tree—The Holy Tree of Bostam—The Bygas of the Eastern Sathpuras—Tree Worship in Mysore—The Palm Tree—Worship of the Palm at Najran—The Tree of Ten Thousand Images—Tree Worship in Persia—Sacred Old Testament Trees—The Classics—Forests and Groves favourite places of Worship—Origin of Groves—Votive Offerings to Trees.

CHAPTER III. 32

    Arab Tree Worship—Story of Kaimun, the captive slave—Miracle of the Date Tree—Persian bushes—Plane-tree—The Great Cypress—The old man of Diarbekir—The Fervüers—Anecdote of Xerxes—Anecdote of a merchant and his wife—The bush of the "Excellent" Tree—The Cypresses of the Zoroaster—Motawakel—The Triple-tree of Abraham—Tree of the Club of Hercules—The Tree of Passienus Crispus—The Virgin Mary's Fig-tree—Tree of Mohammed's Staff—The Neema-tree of the Gallas—Irish Superstitions—Saint Valeri—People of Livonia—Destruction of a Sacred Tree.

CHAPTER IV. 44

    The Bogaha of Ceylon, or God-tree—The Maha Wanse and the Bo-tree—Ceremonies connected with the transplantation of the Bo-tree—Planting the great Bo-branch—Miracles of the Bo-tree—The State Elephant—The Pipal Tree.

viii. CONTENTS.

PAGE.

CHAPTER V. 58

Sacred Trees very ancient in Egypt—Hebrew Trees—The Sycamore at Mataren—Ionic Forms—The Koran on Mary and the Palm-tree—Sacredness of the Palm in Egypt—Tree Worship in Dahome—The Sacred Tree of the Canary Isles.

CHAPTER VI. 64

Usefulness of the Ash-tree—Its position among Sacred Trees—The Queen of Trees—Mythology of the Ash—Scotch Superstitious Usages—The "Ash Faggot Ball" of Somersetshire—Pliny and others on the Serpent and the Ash—The Ash as a medium of cure of complaints—Anecdotes—Phallic Associations—The New-birth—Ireland and the Ash—The Juniper-Tree—The Madonna and the Juniper—The Elm-tree—Mythology of the Elm—The Apple-tree—Mythological allusions to the Apple-tree—The Pine-tree—Wind Spirits—German Superstitions—The Oak-tree—Universal Sacredness of the Oak—The Oak of the Hebrew Scriptures—Classic Oaks—Socrates and his Oath—Greek Sayings—The Trees Speaking—Sacred Ash of Dodona—Legend of Philemon and Baucis—The Hamadryads—The Yule Log—St. Boniface—Mysteries connected with the Oak—Christmas-trees.

CHAPTER VII. 85

Icelandic Customs—The Sacred Ash—The Prose Edda and Tree Worship—Icelandic Mythology of the Ash—The Norns—The Czeremissa of the Wolga—The Jakuhti—Sacred Trees of Livonia—Phallic Tree Worship and objects in Bavaria.

TREE WORSHIP.

CHAPTER I.

Characteristics of Trees—Naturalness of Tree Worship—Origin of the Worship—The Tree of Life—Ancient Types—A Tree as a Symbol of Life—Poetical Associations—Sacred Fig Tree—India specially a Land of Tree Worship—Trees identified with Gods — Meritoriousness of Planting Trees — Auspicious and Inauspicious Trees—Ceremonies connected with Tree Worship—Invocations of Tree Gods—Banian Tree—Ritual Directions—Santal Worship.

IN contemplating the various objects to which men, in their efforts to construct a natural and satisfactory religion, have rendered divine honour and worship, it is not surprising to find that trees, flowers, and shrubs have shared largely in this adoration. While it was possible to offer such a tribute to mere stocks and stones and the works of men's hands, the transition to trees and their floral companions would be an easy one. Most people will agree with the statement, often made, that "There are few of the works of nature that combine so many and so varied charms and beauties as a forest; that whether considered generally or particularly, whether as a grand geographical feature of a country or as a collection of individual trees, it is alike invested with beauty and with interest, and opens up to the mind a boundless field for inquiry into the mysterious laws of creation. But a forest is not merely an aggregate of trees, it is not merely a great embodiment of vegetable life: it is the cheerful and pleasant abode of numerous varieties of animal life, who render it more animated and picturesque, and who find there shelter, food, and happy homes."

"There is, perhaps, no object in nature that adds so much to the beauty, that, in fact, may be said to be a necessary ingredient in the beauty of a landscape, as a tree.

A tree, indeed, is the highest and noblest production of the vegetable kingdom, just as man holds the highest place in the animal. Whether standing solitary, or arranged in clumps, or masses, or avenues, trees always give freshness, variety, and often grandeur to the scene.

"Unless a man be a forester or a timber contractor by profession, he cannot walk through a forest in spring without having his mind stored with new ideas and with good and happy thoughts. Here is an entirely new animated world opened up to his admiring gaze; a world that seems to be innocent and pure, for everything in it is rejoicing and glad. The first glow and flush of life visible all around is so vigorous and strong, that man partakes of its vigour and strength. He, too, feels an awakening of new life, not of painful but of pleasant sensations; on every side his eye falls on some form of beauty or of grandeur, and they quietly impress pictures on his mind never to be effaced, for

'A thing of beauty is a joy for ever.'"*

It is easy, therefore, to understand how in times and places where men in their efforts to adore a Supreme Being, worshipped the beauties and wonders of creation, trees should become the representatives of the Divine if not actually the gods themselves. "The sun as the source of light and warmth, the changes of the seasons, the growth of herbage, flowers and trees, great rivers and oceans, mountains and deep glens—in short whatever of the works of nature is most beautiful or awful, and acts upon the intellectual or sensual perceptions, naturally becomes the object of adoration. Among these objects trees took an early place. Their beauty when single, their grandeur as forests, their grateful shade in hot climates, their mysterious forms of life, suggested them as the abodes of departed spirits, or of existing agencies of the Creator. If the solemn gloom of deep forests and groves were consecrated to the most awful of holy and unholy mysteries, the more open woodland glades became in imagination peopled with nymphs, dryads, and fauns, and contributed to the most joyous portions of adorative devotion. Thus the abstract sacred character of trees is not difficult to conceive, and as the intellect progressed among

* "English Forests and Forest Trees."

the early races of the world, we can follow among the Greeks and the Aryans, as well as the Hebrews, its naturally poetic and sacred development."*

Serpent worship is by no means so easy to account for as tree worship, but it is a fact that in many places the two were intimately associated; having dealt with the first of these in a former volume, we now exclusively treat of the latter. Speaking of the naturalness of tree worship, Fergusson pertinently remarks—"Where we miss the point of contact with our own religious notion is when we ask how anyone could hope that a prayer addressed to a tree was likely to be responded to, or how an offering presented to such an object could be appreciated. Originally it may have been that a divinity was supposed to reside among the branches, and it was to this spirit that the prayer was first addressed; but anyone who has watched the progress of idolatry must have observed how rapidly minds, at a certain stage of enlightenment, weary of the unseen, and how wittingly they transfer their worship to any tangible or visible object. An image, a temple, a stone or tree may thus become an object of adoration or of pilgrimage, and when sanctified by time, the indolence of the human mind too gladly contents itself with any idol which previous generations have been content to venerate."

"For the origin of the mysterious reverence with which certain trees and flowers were anciently regarded, and of tree 'worship,' properly so called, we must go back to that primæval period into which comparative mythology has of late afforded us such remarkable glimpses; when the earth to its early inhabitants seemed 'apparelled in celestial light,' but when every part of creation seemed to be endowed with a strange and conscious vitality. When rocks and mountains, the most apparently lifeless and unchanging of the world's features, were thus regarded and were personified in common language, it would have been wonderful if the more life-like plains—the great rivers that fertilised, and the trees with their changing growth and waving branches that clothed them—should have been disregarded and unhonoured. Accordingly sacred ruins and sacred trees appear in the very earliest mythologies which have been recovered, and linger amongst the last vestiges of heathenism long after the advent of a purer creed. Either as direct objects of worship, or as forming the temple under whose solemn shadow other and remoter deities might be adored, there is no part of the world in which trees have not been regarded with especial reverence:—

> 'In such green palaces the first kings reigned;
> Slept in their shade, and angels entertained.
> With such cold counsellors they did advise,
> And by frequenting sacred shades, grew wise.'

Paradise itself, says Evelyn, was but a kind of "nemorous temple or sacred grove," planted by God himself, and given to man; and he goes on to suggest that the groves which the patriarchs are recorded to have planted in different parts of Palestine, may have been memorials of that first tree-shaded paradise from which Adam was expelled.

"How far the religious systems of the great nations of antiquity were affected by the record of the Creation and Fall preserved in the opening chapters of Genesis, is not perhaps possible to determine. There are certain points of resemblance which are at least remarkable, but which we may assign, if we please, either to independent tradition, or to a natural development from the mythology of the earliest or primæval period. The Trees of Life and of Knowledge are at once suggested by the mysterious sacred tree which appears in the most ancient sculptures and paintings of Egypt and Assyria, and in those of the remoter East. In the symbolism of these nations the sacred tree sometimes figures as a type of the universe, and represents the whole system of created things, but more frequently as a 'tree of life,' by whose fruit the votaries of the gods are nourished with divine strength, and one prepared for the joys of immortality. The most ancient types of this mystical tree of life are the date, the fig, and the pine or cedar. Of these, the earliest of which any representation occurs is the palm—the true date palm of the valley of the Nile and of the great alluvial plain of ancient Babylonia—a tree which is exceeded in size and dignity by many of its congeners, but which is spread over two, at least, of the great centres of ancient civilization, and which, besides its great importance as a food producer has a special beauty of its own when the clusters of dates are hanging in golden ripeness under its coronal of dark green leaves. It is figured as a tree of life on an Egyptian sepulchral tablet certainly older than the fifteenth century B.C., and preserved in the museum at Berlin. Two arms issue from the top of the tree, one of which presents a tray of dates to the deceased, who stands in front, whilst the other gives him water, 'the water of life.' The arms are those of the goddess Nepte, who appears at full length in other and later representations."*

Mr. Barlow informs us that the paradise here intended is the state or place of departed righteous souls, who, according to Egyptian theology as explained in the works of Rossellini, Wilkinson, Lepsius, Birch, and Emmanuel de Rougè, have triumphed over evil through the power of Osiris, whose name they bear, and are now set down for ever in his heavenly kingdom. Osiris was venerated as the incarnation of the goddess of the Deity, and according to the last-mentioned authority, was universally worshipped in Egypt as the Redeemer of souls two thousand years before Christ.

The head of this family was named Poer, and the members of it are shown seated in two rows on thorns, one below the other; each is receiving from the Tree of Life, or rather from the divine influence residing in the tree, and personified as a vivifying agent under the figure of the goddess Nupte or Nepte, a stream of the life-giving water, and at the same time an offering of its fruit. The tree is the *ficus-sycamorous*, the sycamore tree of the Bible, and it stands on a sort of aquarium, symbolical of the sacred Nile, the life-supporting agent in the land of Egypt. The tree is abundantly productive, and from the upper part of it, among the branches, the goddess Nepte rises with a tray of fruit in one hand, and with the other pours from a vase streams of its life-giving water.

Mr. Barlow further says—"In the 'Tree of Life' of the Egyptians, we have perhaps the earliest, certainly the most complete and consistent representation of this most ancient and seemingly universal symbol, the Tree of Life, in the midst of paradise, furnishing the divine support of immortality." †

Forlong says—"In his little work on Symbolism, under

---

* See *Quar. Rev.*, 114. † " Symbolism."

the head '*Sacred Trees*,' Mr. Barlow has expressed what I have long felt. He says, 'the most *generally received symbol of life* is a tree, as also the most appropriate. . . . There might be an innate appreciation of the beautiful and the grand in this impression, conjoined with the conception of a more sublime truth, and *the first principles of a natural theology*, but in most instances it would appear rather to have been the result of an ancient and primitive *symbolical* worship, *at one time universally prevalent.*" (The italics are Forlong's.) As men came to recognise in themselves two natures—the physical and spiritual, the life of the body and the life of the soul—"So these came to be represented either by two trees, as sometimes found, or in reference to universal life, by one tree only." Some thousands of years before even the age *imputed* to Genesis, there were sculptured on the Zodiac of Dendera, Egypt, two sacred trees, the Western and Eastern; the first was *truth* and *religion* —the sacred palm surmounted by the ostrich feather—the latter, the *vital or generative force of nature*, beyond which Egypt thought she had risen, therein surpassing her Eastern parent; at least so I feel inclined to class them chronologically. "Besides the monumental evidence furnished," says Barlow, "of a sacred tree, a Tree of Life, there is an historical and traditional evidence of the same thing found in the early literature of various nations, in their customs and usages." All grand, extraordinary, beautiful, or highly useful trees, have in every land at some time been associated with the noble, wonderful, lovely and beneficial ideas which man has attributed to his God or to nature. We can recognise the early worship of trees in the reverence of thought which attaches to the two in the centre of man's first small world, a garden of fruits and shade. "All unhistorical though the tales may be," continues Forlong, "there is a deep poetry underlying the story of the sacred garden. We naturally picture it as a 'grove,' for man was not yet a cultivator of the ground; amidst the deep shades of Eden, we are told, walked the great Elohim with the man and woman —naked—as created by him through his Logos, *Ruach*, Spirit, or Spouse, but yet 'without the knowledge' which 'the sacred tree of knowledge' was soon to impart."

Further on Forlong remarks—"The numerous tales of holy trees, groves and gardens repeated everywhere and in every possible form, fortify me in my belief that tree worship *was first known*, and after it came Lingam or Phallic, with, of course, its female form Adāma."

"The serpent being Passion, and symbolic of the second faith, followed, we may say, almost simultaneously; thus we find the sacred garden-groves of all Edens first mentioned, then the instructor, the serpent, and latterly creative powers in Adām and Adāma, or in Asher and Ashera, which last female worship the Old Testament translators call the 'Grove.' We are told it was always set up with Asher, Babel, &c., under 'every green tree' by ancient Israel, and up to a few hundred years before Christ, and not seldom even after Christ.

"All Eastern literature teems with the stories told of and under the sacred fig tree, *Ficus Religiosa*, Gooler, a *Ficus Indica*. Under its holy shade, gods, goddesses, men and animals disport themselves, and talk with each other on sacred and profane themes. From it, as from many another holy tree, ascended gods and holy men to heaven, and it and many others are to be yet the cradles of coming Avatars. To the present hour we find thousands of barren women still worshipping and giving offerings throughout the year to this Peepal, or male fig tree of India, to obtain offspring: nor is the female tree, the *Ficus Indica*, neglected; at stated periods this Băr, or true Bānian, must be also worshipped with offerings by all who wish such boons. Under this sacred tree did the pious *Săkyamooni* become a *Boodh*, or enlightened one; and it is from the rubbing together of the wood of trees, notably of the three Banian trees—Peepal, Băr, and Gooler *(Ficus Sycamores), the favourite woods for Phallic images*, that holy fire is drawn from heaven, and before all these species do women crave their desires from God."

With regard to the Ficus, Forlong remarks that others besides Jews have seen divers reasons why it is said to have been the first covering used by the human race. "The symbolic trefoil or *fleur de lys* with its seed springing from its stems, is still used as a Phallic ornament, and the leaf, especially of the Bo, is very like the old form of Ph: it has a long attenuated point, and is ever quivering on the stillest days. The tree has many peculiarities, not only in its leaves and modes of leafing, but in its fruit and modes of multiplying, which could not fail to make it of a very holy and important character in the pious, poetical and imaginative mind of the East. Among others the fruit or seed hangs direct from its limbs, yet it is commonly said to be germinated by seed from heaven; birds carry off the seed and deposit it on all high places, and in the trunks of other trees; these this Ficus splits asunder and entwines itself all around, descending by the parent trunk as well as aerially, by dropping suckers until it reaches *Mother-Earth*, by which time it has most likely killed the parent tree, which has up to that period nourished it. Thus the Ficus tribe is often hollow in the centre, and if the hollow exist near the base, it is always a very holy spot where will usually be found a Lingam or Yoni stone, or both, or a temple of Matra-Deva—Deva or Siva—the great God of Creation."*

"In a country like India, anything that offers a cool shelter from the burning rays of the sun is regarded with a feeling of grateful respect. The wide-spreading Banyan tree is planted and nursed with care, only because it offers a shelter to many a weary traveller. Extreme usefulness of the thing is the only motive perceivable in the careful rearing of other trees. They are protected by religious injunctions, and the planting of them is encouraged by promises of eternal bliss in the future world. The injunction against injuring a banyan or fig tree is so strict, that in the Ramayana even Rávana, an unbeliever, is made to say 'I have not cut down any fig tree, in the month of Vaisakha, why then does the calamity (alluding to the several defeats his army sustained in the war with Rámachandra and to the loss of his sons and brothers) befall me?'"

The medicinal properties of many plants soon attracted notice, and were cultivated with much care. With the illiterate the medicinal virtues of a drug are increased with its scarcity; and to enhance its value it was soon associated with difficulties, and to keep it secret from public knowledge, it was culled in the dark and witching hours of night.

Trees have frequently been identified with gods: thus in the Panma Purána, the religious fig tree is an incarnation of Vishnu, the Indian fig tree of Rudra, and the Palasa of Brahma.

* "Rivers of Life," vol. 1.

In the Varáka Purana, the planter of a group of trees of a particular species is promised heavenly bliss, and it is needless to point out that from the names of the trees recommended, the extensive utility of the act must be acknowledged. Thus it is said, "He never goes to hell who plants an asvatha, or a pichumarda, or a banian, or ten jessamines, or two pomegranates, a panchámra, or five mangoes."

The Tithitatva gives a slightly different list, substituting two champakas, three kesara, seven tala-palms, and nine cocoanuts, instead of the banian, the jessamines, the pomegranates, and the *panchámra*.

As early as the Rámáyana, the planting of a group of trees was held meritorious. The celebrated Panchavati garden where Sitá was imprisoned, has been reproduced by many a religious Hindu, and should any of them not have sufficient space to cultivate the five trees, the custom is to plant them in a small pot where they are dwarfed into small shrubs. Such substitutes and make-shifts are not at all uncommon in the ecclesiastical history of India. In Buddhist India, millions of miniature stone and clay temples, some of them not higher than two inches, were often dedicated when more substantial structures were not possible. The Panchavati consists of the asvatha planted on the east side, the vilva or *Ægle marmelos* on the north, the banian on the west, the *Emblica officinalis* on the south, and the asoka on the south-east.

The Skanda Purána recommends a vilva in the centre, and four others on four sides; four banians in four corners, twenty-five asokas in a circle, with a myrobalan on one side, as the constituents of a great punchavati.

Superstition has always been active in drawing nice distinctions between the auspicious and the inauspicious, and it is curious to observe how the auspicious qualities of some plants have been extolled. Some are considered auspicious when planted near a dwelling house.

No tree with fruit or blossoms can be cut down, as the sloka threatens the cutter with destruction of his family and wealth. Therefore never cut down any tree that bears good flowers or fruits if you desire the increase of your family, of your wealth and of your future happiness.

Superstition has associated supernatural properties with many plants, and several have been identified with the gods.

The *durvá*, a kind of grass very common in all parts of India, is excellent food for cattle. It is an essential article in the worship of all gods. It is said to have originated from the thigh of Vishnu.

The religious fig tree makes one rich, the *Jonesia Asoka* destroys all sorrow, the *Ficus Venosa* is said to be useful in sacrifices, and the *Nim* gives much happiness. *Syzygium Jambolanum* promises heavenly bliss, and the pomegranate a good wife. *Ficus glomerata* cures diseases, and *Butea frondosa* gives the protection of Brahma. The *Calotropis gigantea* is useful as it pleases the sun, every day the bel tree pleases *Siva*, and the *Patalá* pleases *Párvati*. The Asparas are pleased with *Bombax malabaricum*, and the Gandharvas with Jasminum, the *Terminalia* chebula increases the number of servants, and the *Mimusops elenchi* gives maid-servants. The *Tál* is injurious to children, and the Mimusops elenchi productive of large families. The cocoanut gives many wives, and the vine gives a beautiful body; the *Corolia latifolia* increases desires, and the Pandanus odoratissimum destroys all. The tamarind tree is considered most inauspicious, and according to the *Vaidya Sastras*, is very injurious to health. The *Carica papeya* plant is more so. The Sunflower, Helianthus, is supposed to emit gases that destroy miasma.

The following trees are said to have peculiar virtues. The Indian fig tree, if on the east side of a house, is always auspicious; so also is the Udumvava tree if on the west, and the pipul if on the south, &c.

The following are supposed to have a peculiar influence on particular spots. The cocoanut tree near the dwelling-house confers wealth on the family, and if on the east or north-east of an encampment, the tree is the donor of sons. The mango tree, the best of trees, is auspicious at every place, and if situated on the east, gives wealth to men. The *Bel* tree, the jack tree, and the citron tree, and the plum tree, are in all situations conducive to prosperity.

The *Durvashtami* is one of the many vratas observed by Hindu females. It is celebrated on the eighth lunar day of the bright fortnight of the month of Bhádro. On the day fixed for worshipping Durvá a fast is observed, and Durvá, Gauri, Ganesá and Siva are worshipped with rice, fruits and flowers. Durvá is described as dark as the petals of a blue lotus, held on the heads of all the gods, pure, born from the body of Vishnu, anointed with nectar, free from all sickness, immortal, incarnation of Vishnu, and giver of good children, and virtue, wealth and salvation.

A thread with eight knots, and fruits, &c., are presented to Durvá, and the following prayer is then read—

"Durvá, you are called immortal, and you are worshipped both by gods and asuras. Having blessed us with prosperity and children, fulfil all our wishes. As you extend over the earth with your suckers and branches, in the same way give me healthy and immortal children."

After the usual puja, the thread with eight knots is tied on the left arm and the worshipper listens to the legend of Durvá repeated by the officiating priest.

The Asokáshtami, the Arunvdaya Saptami, and the Madanotsava, are three other vratas in which trees are worshipped.

From the Sakrotthana, the rising of India after the new moon preceding the Durgá-puja, the whole fortnight is devoted to one or other form of tree worship. Asokashtami is observed on the eighth day of the bright fortnight of Chaitra.

In the month of Chaitra on the thirteenth lunar day, the Madanotsava is celebrated and the Asoka tree is worshipped.

But the most important instance of tree worship is the Durgápujá. Although the festival is a rejoicing at the promising crops in the field, and although it may be traced to the solar myth and Ushá or dawn worship, it is undoubtedly one of the most extensive festivals of tree worship.

Along with the goddess Durgá, the *Nava* patrici or the nine leaves are worshipped.

On the morning of the first day of the puja, nine branches with leaves are tied together with a plant of *Clitoria ternata alba*, and a twig bearing a pair of fruits with suitable mantras, is stuck in the bundle. Before cutting the twig, the following mantras are repeated—

"Sriphala tree, you are born on the mountain Mandar, Meru Kailsa, and at the top of the Himavat, you are always a favourite of Ambica. Born on the top of the Scri hill Sriphala! You are the resting place of prosperity, I take you away to worship you as Durgá herself.

"Om Vilva tree, most prosperous, always a favourite

of Sankara, I worship the devi, having taken away your branch. O Lord, you must not mind the pain generated by the separation of your branch. I bow to the Vilva tree born on the Hymalaya mountain, favourite of Parvasa and embraced by Siva. You are auspicious in action and a favourite of Bhagavati; for the sake of Bhavani's words, give me all success." The bundle is then anointed with various cosmetics and aromatic drugs and oils, and is placed by the side of the idols. The several plants are then separately invoked, and the goddesses presiding over each are worshipped.

The following are the mantras for worshipping them :—

"Om, salutation be to Brāhmani, the goddess dwelling in the plantain tree. Om, Devi Durga, welcome, come near us. In the Brahma form distribute peace to all. Om, salutations be to you.

"Om, salutation be to Kalika, the goddess dwelling in the Arum plant. Om, good-natured in the war of Mahisha dema, you became arum plant. Om, the beloved of Hara, come hither for my blessing.

"Om, salutation be to Durga, the goddess dwelling in the turmeric plant. Om, Haridra, you are Hara incarnate. Om, good-natured you are Umá incarnate. For the destruction of my ill-luck do receive my pujá and be propitiated.

"Om, salutation be to Kartika, the goddess dwelling in the Sesvania plant. Om, during the destruction of Sumbha and Nisumbha demons, goddess of success, you were worshipped by India and all gods. Be pleased with us.

"Om, salutation be to Sivá, the goddess dwelling in the vilva tree. Om, beloved of Mahadeva and beloved of Vishnu, beloved of Umá, vilva tree salute you.

"Om, salutation be to Raktadantika (blood-teethed), the goddess dwelling in the pomegranate tree. Om, formerly in the war, you became Dádimi in the presence of Raktavija demon, you acted the part of Umá, therefore bless us.

"Om, salutation be to Sokarahita (devoid of sorrow), the goddess dwelling in the Asoka tree. Om, Asoka tree, you please Siva and you destroy all sorrow. Make me sorrowless in the same way as you please Durvá.

"Om, salutation be to Chámundá, the goddess dwelling in the Man tree. Om, on whose leaves rests the Devi, beloved of Sachi, for my prosperity receive my pujá.

"Om, salutations be to Lakshmi, the goddess dwelling in the rice plant. Om, for the preservation of the life of all beings you were created by Brahma. Om, preserve me in the same way as you please Umá." (See the Vastu Yaga and its bearings upon Tree and Serpent Worship in India, by Pratapachandra Ghosha).

The Banian or Indian fig tree, is perhaps the most beautiful and surprising production of nature in the vegetable kingdom. Some of these trees are of an amazing size, and as they are always increasing, they may in some measure be said to be exempt from decay. Every branch proceeding from the trunk throws out its own roots, first in small fibres, at the distance of several yards from the ground. These, continually becoming thicker as they approach the earth, take root and shoot out new branches, which in time bend downwards, take root in the like manner, and produce other branches, which continue in this state of progression as long as they find soil to nourish them.

The Hindoos are remarkably fond of this tree, for they look upon it as an emblem of the Deity, on account of its out-stretching arms and its shadowy beneficence. They almost pay divine honours, and "find a Fane in every Grove."

Near these trees the most celebrated pagodas are generally erected; the Brahmins spend their lives in religious solitude under their friendly shade, and the natives of all castes and tribes are fond of retreating into the cool recesses and natural bowers of this umbrageous canopy, which is impervious to the fiercest beams of the tropical sun.

The particular tree here described grows on an island in the river Nerbedda, ten miles from the city of Baroach, in the province of Guzzurat, a flourishing settlement formerly in possession of the East India Company, but ceded by the government of Bengal at the treaty of peace concluded with the Mahrattas in 1783, to Mahadjee, a Mahratta chief.

This tree, called in India *Cubeer Burr*, in honour of a famous saint, was much larger than it has been of late; for high floods have at different times carried away the banks of the island where it grows, and along with such parts of the tree as had extended their roots thus far; yet what has remained is about two thousand feet in circumference, measuring round the principal stems; but the hanging branches, the roots of which have not yet reached the ground, cover a much larger extent. The chief trunks of this single tree amount to three hundred and fifty, all superior in size to the generality of our English oaks and elms; the smaller stems, forming into stronger supports, are more than three thousand; and from each of these new branches, hanging roots are proceeding, which in time will form trunks and become parents to a future progeny.

Cubeer Burr is famed throughout Hindostan for its prodigious extent, antiquity and great beauty. The Indian armies often encamp around it; and, at certain seasons, solemn Jattras or Hindoo festivals are held here, to which thousands of votaries repair from various parts of the Mogul empire. Seven thousand persons, it is said, may easily repose under its shade. There is a tradition among the natives, that this tree is three thousand years old; and there is great reason to believe it, and that it is this amazing tree that Arrian describes when speaking of the gymosophists in his book of Indian affairs. These people, he says, in summer wear no clothing. In winter they enjoy the benefit of the sun's rays in the open air; and in summer, when the heat becomes excessive, they pass their time in moist and marshy places under large trees, which according to Nearchus, cover a circumference of five acres, and extend their branches so far that ten thousand men may easily find shelter under them.

English gentlemen, when on hunting and shooting parties, are accustomed to form extensive encampments, and to spend several weeks under this delightful pavilion of foliage, which is generally filled with a great variety of feathered songsters. This tree not only affords shelter but sustenance to all its inhabitants; being loaded with small figs of a rich scarlet colour.*

Trees have always been among the chief divinities of India. In the "Institutes of Menu," chap. 3, we find directions to the Brahman for his oblations, and, after a number of preliminaries, the injunctions proceed—" Having thus, with fixed attention, offered clarified butter in all quarters, proceeding from the east in a southerly direction, to India, Yama, Varuna, and the god Soma, let him offer his gifts to animated creatures, saying, I salute the Maruts

* "Indian Antiquities."

or Winds, let him throw dressed rice near the door, saying, I salute the water-gods, in water; and on his pestle and mortar, saying, I salute the gods of large trees."

An instance of tree worship amongst the Santals or hill tribes of Beerbhoom is recorded in Hunter's "Annals of Rural Bengal," as follows—"Adjoining the Santal village is a grove of their natural tree, the Sal (Shorea Robusta), which they believe to be the favourite resort of all the family gods of the little community. From its silent gloom the bygone generations watch their children and children's children playing their several parts in life, not altogether with an unfriendly eye. Nevertheless the ghastly inhabitants of the grove are sharp critics, and deal out crooked limbs, cramps and leprosy, unless duly appeased. Several times a year the whole hamlet, dressed out in its showiest, repairs to the grove to do honour to the *Lares Rurales* with music and sacrifice. Men and women join hands, and, dancing in a large circle, chant songs in remembrance of the original founder of the community who is venerated as the head of the village Pantheon. Goats, red cocks, and chickens are sacrificed; and while some of the worshippers are told off to cook the flesh for the common festival at great fires, the rest separate into families and dance round the particular trees which they fancy their domestic Lares chiefly inhabit. Among the more superstitious tribes, it is customary for each family to dance round every single tree, in order that they may not by any chance omit the one in which their gods may be residing."

CHAPTER II.

The Bael Tree—Worship of the Left Hand—Trees of the Sun and Moon—The Arbre Sec or Dry Tree—The Holy Tree of Bostam—The Bygas of the Eastern Sathpuras—Tree Worship in Mysore—The Palm Tree—Worship of the Palm at Najrau—The Tree of Ten Thousand Images—Tree Worship in Persia—Sacred Old Testament Trees—The Classics — Forests and Groves, favourite Places of Worship—Origin of Groves—Votive Offerings to Trees.

"THE Bael Tree," says Forlong, "as a representative of the triad and monad, is always offered at Lingam worship, after washing the Lingam with water and anointing it with sandal wood. The god is supposed to specially like all white flowers and cooling embrocations, which last sandal wood is held to be; and he is very commonly to be found under an umbrageous Bael, more especially if there be no fine Ficus near; failing both, the poor god is often reduced to the stump of a tree; and if that is also scarce, his votaries raise to him a karn or cairn of stones, with the prominent one in the centre, and plant a pomegranate, bits of tolsi, &c., near; and if water is available, a little garden of flowers, of which the marigolds are a favourite. My readers must not fancy that this worship is indecent, or even productive of licentiousness. It is conducted by men, women and children of modest mien, and pure and spotless lives, though at certain seasons, as in all faiths and lands, the passions are roused and the people proceed to excesses, yet Sivaism is peculiarly free from this with reference to others, not excluding Eastern Christianity. Vishnooism, which we may call the worship of *The Left Hand,* or female energies, is perhaps the greatest sinner in this respect. Sivaism is for the most part *harshly ascetic,* as regards its office-bearers and orthodox followers; yet all faiths give way at certain solar periods, and all Hindoo sects are as bad as Romans at the spring 'hilaria or carnival,' the more so if Ceres or Kybele is propitious, and more apparently so in countries where writings have not yet supplanted pictures. Amongst all the rudest tribes of India, and even throughout Rajpootana, and with the strict Jain sects who abhor Lingam worship, these still shew their parent root by devoting some fifteen days annually, after the harvests are gathered in, to the most gross form of Lingam worship, in which a complete naked image of a man, called 'Elajee,' is built of clay and decorated with wreaths of flowers, &c., and placed in prominent situations. In most parts of Rajpootana, this male image exists at every city and village gate, but it is not rendered conspicuously indecent until the hooly or harvest enjoyments; and low and degrading as these are, reminding us of our purely animal frame, yet no Hindoo practices of harvest times are so gross as I have seen practised at the harvest homes or midnight revelries of our own country."

The oracular trees of the Sun and Moon, somewhere on the confines of India, appear in all the fabulous histories of Alexander from the Pseudo-Callisthenes downwards. Thus Alexander is made to tell the story—"Then came some of the townspeople and said, 'We have to show thee something passing strange, O King, and worth thy visiting; for we can show thee trees that talk with human speech.' So they led me to a certain park, in the midst of which were the Sun and Moon, and round about them a guard of priests of the Sun and Moon. And there stood the two trees of which they had spoken, like unto cypress trees; and round about them were trees like the myrobolans of Egypt, and with similar fruit. And I addressed the two trees that were in the midst of the park, the one which was male in the masculine gender, and the one that was female in the feminine gender. And the name of the male tree was the Sun, and of the female tree the Moon, names which were in that language Muthu and Emaüsae. And the stems were clothed with the skins of animals; the male tree with the skins of he-beasts, and the female tree with the skins of she-beasts. . . . And at the setting of the Sun a voice, speaking in the Indian tongue, came forth from the (Sun) tree; and I ordered the Indians who were with me to interpret it. But they were afraid and would not."

Maundeville informs us precisely where the trees are—"A fifteen journeys in lengthe, goyinge be the deserts of the tother side of the Ryvere Beumare," if one could only tell where that is. A mediæval chronicler also tells us that Ogerus, the Dane (*temp. Caroli Magni*), conquered all the parts beyond sea from Hierusalem to the Trees of the Sun. In the old Italian romance also of *Guerino detto il Meschino*, still a chap book in south Italy, the hero visits the Trees of the Sun and Moon.

It will be observed that the letter ascribed to Alexander describes the two oracular trees as resembling two cypress trees. As such the Trees of the Sun and Moon are represented on several extant ancient medals, *e.g.*, on two struck at Perga, in Pamphylia, in the time of Aurelian. An Eastern story tells us of two vast cypress trees, sacred among the Magians, which grew in Khorasan, one at Kashmar near Turshiz, and the other at Farmad near Tuz, and which were said to have risen from shoots that Zoroaster brought from paradise. The former of these was sacrilegiously cut down by the order of the Khalif Motawakkil, in the ninth century. The trunk was dispatched to Baghdad on rollers at a vast expense, whilst the branches alone formed a load for 1,300 camels. The night that the convoy reached within one stage of the palace, the Khalif was cut in pieces by his own guards. This tree was said to be 1,450 years old, and to measure $33\frac{3}{4}$ cubits in girth. The locality of this "Arbol Sol" we see was in Khorasan, and possibly its fame may have been transferred to a representative of another species. The plane as well as the cypress was one of the distinctive trees of the Magian paradise.

In the Peutingerian Tables we find in the north-east of Asia the rubric, "*Hic Alexander Responsum accepit,*" which looks very like an allusion to the tale of the Oracular Trees. If so, it is remarkable as a suggestion of the antiquity of the Alexandrian legends, though the rubric may of course be an interpolation. The Trees of the Sun and Moon appear as located in India Ultima to the east of Persia, in a map which is found in MSS. (12th century) of the *Floridus of Lambertus*; and they are indicated more or less precisely in several maps of the succeeding centuries.

Marco has mixed up this legend of the Alexandrian romance on the authority, as we have reason to believe, of some of the re-compilers of that romance, with a famous subject of *Christian* legend in that age, the Arbre Sec or

Dry Tree, one form of which is related by Maundeville and by Johan Schiltberger. "A lytille fro Ebron," says the former, "is the Mount of Mambre, of the whyche the Valeye taketh his name. And there is a tree of Oke that the Saracens clepen Dirpe, that is of Abraham's Tyme, the which men clepen the Dry Tree. And theye saye that it hath ben this sithe the beginnynge of the World; and was sumtyme grene and bare Leves, unto the Tyme that Oure Lord dyede on the Cross; and thanne it dryede; and so dyden alle the Trees that weren thanne in the World. And summe seyn he here Prophecyes that a Lord, a Prynce of the West syde of the World, shall wynnen the Land of Promyssioum, i.e. the Holy Land, withe Helpe of Cristene Men, and he halle do synge a Masse under that Drye Tree, and than the Tree shall wexen grene and bere both Fruyt and Leves. And thorghe that Myracle manye Sarazines and Jewes schulle hev turned to Cristene Feithe. And, therefore, they dan gret Worschippe thereto, and kepen it fulle besyly. And alle be it so that it be drye, natheloss yet be herethe great vertu, &c."

The tradition seems to have altered with circumstances, for a traveller of nearly two centuries later (Friar Anselmo, 1590), describes the oak of Abraham at Hebron as a tree of dense and verdant foliage:—"The Saracens make their devotions at it, and hold it in great veneration, for it has remained thus green from the days of Abraham until now; and they tie scraps of cloth on its branches inscribed with some of their writing, and believe that if any one were to cut a piece off that tree he would die within the year." Indeed, even before Maundeville's time, Friar Burchard (1283) had noticed that though the famous old tree was dry, another had sprung from its roots.

As long ago as the time of Constantine a fair was held under the Terebink of Maimre, which was the object of many superstitious rites and excesses. The Emperor ordered these to be put a stop to, and a church to be erected on the spot. In the time of Arculph (end of 7th century), the dry trunk still existed under the roof of this church.

There are several Dry Tree stories among the wonders of Buddhism; one is that of a sacred tree visited by the Chinese pilgrims to India, which had grown from the twig which Sakya in Hindu fashion had used as a tooth-brush; and I think there is a like story in our own country of the Glastonbury Thorn having grown from the staff of Joseph of Arimathea.

He who injured the holy tree of Bostam, we are told, perished the same day; a general belief in regard to those *Trees of Grace* of which we have already seen instances in regard to the sacred trees of Zoroaster and the Oak of Hebron. We find the same belief in Eastern Africa, where certain trees, regarded by the natives with superstitious reverence, which they express by driving in votive nails and suspending rags, are known to the European residents by the vulgar name of *Devil Trees*. Burton relates a case of the verification of the superstition in the death of an English merchant who had cut down such a tree, and of four members of his household. (See note on p. 120 of Yule's "Marco Polo's Travels," vol I.)

The writer of an article in the *Cornhill Magazine* of November, 1874, on the Gonds and Bygas of the Eastern Sathpuras (Central Provinces, India), says—

"My endeavours to obtain a clear insight into their ways were so far successful, that after a time they did not object to my being present at their domestic ceremonies, and gradually the Byga priests supplied me with all the information they could give as to their curious custom of tree culture and spirit worship.

"All that they could tell did not throw much light on the subject, for even to the Bygas themselves it is extremely vague and mysterious; but the contrast between their acknowledged hatred of trees as a rule, and their deep veneration of certain others in particular, is very curious.

"I have seen hill-sides swept clear of forests for miles, with but here and there a solitary tree left standing. These remain now the objects of the deepest veneration, and receive offerings of food, clothes, or flowers from the passing Byga, who firmly believes that tree to be the home of a spirit."

Captain J. S. F. Mackenzie, some years ago, contributed a paper to the *Indian Antiquary* on Tree and Serpent Worship in Mysore. He said that round about Bangalose, more especially the Lal Bagh and Petta—as the native town is called—three or more stones are to be found together, having representations of serpents carved upon them. These stones are erected always under the sacred fig tree, by some pious persons, whose means and piety determine the care and finish with which they are executed. Judging from the number of the stones, the worship of the serpent appears to be more prevalent in the Bungalose district than in other parts of the province. No priest is ever in charge of them. There is no objection to men doing so, but, from the custom or from some reason—partly because the serpent is supposed to confer fertility on barren women—the worshipping of the stones, which takes place during the Gauri feast, is confined to women of all Hindu classes and creeds. The stones, when properly erected, ought to be on a built-up stone platform facing the rising sun, and under the shade of two *peepul* (*ficus religiosa*) trees— a male and female growing together, and wedded by ceremonies in every respect the same as in the case of human beings —close by, and growing in the same platform a *nimb* (*margosa*) and *bipatra* (a kind of wood-apple), which are supposed to be living witnesses of the marriage. The expense of performing the marriage ceremony is too heavy for ordinary persons, and so we generally find only one *peepul* and a *nimb* on the platform. By the common people these two are supposed to represent man and wife.

To speak at length of the Palm tree would require a volume—and that a bulky one—rather than a passing notice in a treatise of the most limited dimensions. So much does man owe to this tree in the east, that the inhabitants of those countries where it flourishes can conceive of no land possessing any attraction where it does not exist. An Arab woman lately visiting England once expressed herself to this effect after being shewn everything wonderful that the country had possessed, all in her estimation faded into comparative worthlessness when, in answer to her enquiry, she was told that no palm trees grew there. No tree, in consequence, has been so highly prized or been made so much of. To say that men have been simply grateful for it, or that they have reverenced it, is to stop short of the mark, they have actually deified it and rendered to it divine honours.

"A conventional form of the palm tree occurs on the Nineveh tablets, surrounded by an enclosure of *palmettes*, and attended by winged deities, or ministers holding the *pine-cone* symbol of life, which in Assyrian sculpture takes the place of the *crux-ansata* in the hands of the Egyptian deities.

"The palmette passed from the Assyrians to the Greeks, and formed the crowning ornament of their most beautiful temples. It appears also to have been a symbol among the Etruscans, and, together with the palm tree, will be found on Etruscan sacred utensils."*

Sir William Ousley, from whose travels we quote in other parts of this volume, describes the tree worship at Najran in Arabia, in which the tree was a palm or *Sacred Date*, having its regular priests, festivals, rites and services, and he quotes from a manuscript of the ninth century after Christ, and adds this note from a writer on Indian and Japanese symbols of divinity. "The trunk of a tree on whose top sits Deus the supreme Creator. Some other object might be worthy of observation; but I fix my attention on the *trunk of a tree*. Moreover, whether you go to the Japanese or to the Thibetans, everywhere will meet you *green tree* worship (which has been) transmitted and preserved as symbolic perhaps of the creation and preservation of the world."

This passage, in the opinion of Forlong, shows clearly the Lingam signification of the trunk:—"The Koreish tribe, from which the Arabian prophet sprang, were from earliest known times worshippers of the palm tree, and here, as in other lands, had it been succeeded by the Lingam, and latterly by solar and ancestral worship. The Arabs used to hang on the palm not only garments or pieces of garments, but arms or portions of their warrior gear, thereby showing that they saw in the palm virility—a Herakles or Mercury." †

A very remarkable tree found in Thibet was described by Abbé Huc in his travels in that and other countries in the years 1841-6, it was called the "Tree of Ten Thousand Images," and his account of it is as follows—"The mountain at the foot of which Tsong-Kaba was born, became a famous place of pilgrimage. Lamas assembled there from all parts to build their cells, and thus by degrees was formed

---

* Barlowe's "Symbolism." † Forlong.

that flourishing Lamasery, the fame of which extends to the remotest confines of Tartary. It is called Kounboum, from two Thibetian words signifying Ten Thousand Images, and having allusion to the tree which, according to the legend, sprang from Tsong-Kaba's hair, and bears a Thibetian character on each of its leaves."

"It will here be naturally expected that we say something about this tree itself. Does it exist? Have we seen it? Has it any peculiar attributes? What about its marvellous leaves? All these questions our readers are entitled to put to us. We will endeavour to answer as categorically as possible.

"Yes, this tree does exist, and we had heard of it too often during our journey not to feel somewhat eager to visit it. At the foot of the mountain on which the Lamasery stands, and not far from the principal Buddhist temple, is a great square enclosure formed by brick walls. Upon entering this we were able to examine at leisure the marvellous tree, some of the branches of which had already manifested themselves above the wall. Our eyes were first directed with earnest curiosity to the leaves, and we were filled with an absolute consternation of astonishment at finding that, in point of fact, there were upon each of the leaves well-formed Thibetian characters, all of a green colour, some darker, some lighter than the leaf itself. Our first impression was a suspicion of fraud on the part of the Lamas; but after a minute examination of every detail, we could not discover the least deception. The characters all appeared to us portions of the leaf itself, equally with its veins and nerves; the position was not the same in all; in one leaf they would be at the top of the leaf; in another in the middle; in a third, at the base or at the side; the younger leaves represented the characters only in a partial state of formation. The bark of the tree and its branches, which resemble that of the plane tree, are also covered with these characters. When you remove a piece of old bark, the young bark under it exhibits the indistinct outlines of characters in a germinatory state, and what is very singular, these new characters are not unfrequently different from those which they replace. We examined everything with the closest attention, in order to detect some case of trickery, but we could discern nothing of the sort, and the perspiration absolutely trickled down our faces under the influence of the sensations which this most amazing spectacle created. More profound intellects than ours may, perhaps, be able to supply a satisfactory explanation of the mysteries of this singular tree; but as to us, we altogether give it up. Our readers possibly may smile at our ignorance, but we care not, so that the sincerity and truth of our statement be not suspected.

"The Tree of Ten Thousand Images seemed to us of great age. Its trunk, which three men could scarcely embrace with outstretched arms, is not more than eight feet high; the branches instead of shooting up, spread out in the shape of a plume of feathers, and are extremely bushy; few of them are dead. The leaves are always green; and the wood which has a reddish tint, has an exquisite odour, something like that of cinnamon. The Lamas informed us that in summer, towards the eighth moon, the tree produces large red flowers of an extremely beautiful character. They informed us also that there nowhere else exists another such tree; that various attempts have been made in various Lamaseries of Tartary and Thibet to propagate it by seeds and cuttings, but that all these attempts have been fruitless.

"The Emperor Khang-Hi, when upon a pilgrimage to Kounboum, constructed, at his own private expense, a dome of silver over the Tree of Ten Thousand Images; moreover, he made a present to the Grand Lama of a fine black horse, capable of travelling a thousand lis a day, and of a saddle adorned with precious stones. The horse is dead, but the saddle is still shown in one of the Buddhist temples, where it is an object of special veneration. Before quitting the Lamasery, Khang-Hi endowed it with a yearly revenue for the support of 350 Lamas."

Sir William Ousely says that when in Persia he endeavoured to obtain information from the people respecting the ideas generally formed of Peries or Fairies; imaginary creatures, beautiful and benevolent; also of the Ghúles or "Demons of the Desert," a hideous race, that sometimes haunt cemeteries, and particularly infest a dreary tract in the North of Persia, not far from Teherán, bearing the portentous name of *Melek al mowt dereh*, or "Valley of the Angel of Death." Concerning the *Jins* or Genii, he found they were not restricted to any particular region, but that the gigantic monsters called Dives or Dibes, resided peculiarly among the rocks and forests of *Mazenderan* or Hyrcania.

He then proceeds :—" Those preternatural beings, and others which shall be hereafter mentioned, were the subjects of our conversation when we passed by an old and withered tree half covered with rags, fastened as votive offerings, to the branches; it being one of those entitled by the Persians *dirakht i fázel*, 'excellent or beneficial trees,' and held in superstitious veneration. I had already seen four or five near A'bdúi, and two or three previously in other places, since our departure from Bushehr; and now ascertained that their supposed sanctity did not depend either on the species, the size, or beauty of the trees; nor on their age, although most were old; but often proceeded from accidental, and even trivial circumstances; yet since the reverence paid to trees seemed nearly as ancient, and as widely diffused as any other form of superstition, I have been frequently induced to make it the object of personal inquiry among Asiatics, and of literary research at home. The result now before me would constitute a volume of no inconsiderable size, for the subject may be traced from this present day to the earliest ages of which written records furnish an account; through every country of the old, and, probably, of the new world. The sacred Hebrew scriptures allude to it in many places; we find it mentioned by Greek and Roman authors; various anecdotes respecting it occur in Eastern manuscripts; and it has been noticed by several European travellers and antiquaries."

Further in his work, the same author observes :— " However replete with interesting objects, the ample field of antiquarian research offers but few to our notice under a more attractive form than trees, whether we regard them as distinguishing remarkable spots, the scenes of memorable transactions, as dedicated to certain divinities, or, as in some cases, almost identified with those divinities themselves."

"It is not my intention, nor is it necessary here, to trace back the history of that veneration with which particular trees have been honoured in all ages, and, I believe, in all countries. The Biblical reader will easily recollect many important trees besides that which stood in the midst of the garden of Eden, emphatically styled the 'tree of life,' and the 'tree of knowledge of good and evil.' He will recollect the idolatrous worship in *groves*, and under every *green tree* (Exod. xxxiv. 13, Deut. xvi. 21, &c.) The oak by Shechem, under which Jacob hid all the idols and earrings (Gen. xxxv. 4). The oak near Bethel which marked the grove of Deborah, and was significantly called *Allonbachuth* (Gen. xxxv. 8). The palm tree under which Deborah, the prophetess, dwelt (Judges iv. 5). The oak under which sat 'the man of God' (Kings xiii. 14). The oak in Ophrah, under which the angel of God appeared unto Gideon and conversed with him (Judges vi. 11, 14, 16). The oak that was in the very Sanctuary of the Lord (Joshua xxiv. 26).

"These and other trees which we may suppose lofty and umbrageous, such as the oaks and poplars and elms, because the shadow thereof is good (Hosea iv. 3), must immediately recur to a Biblical reader; but the course of this article will remind him also of that humble bush which the Lord consecrated by his presence, when he revealed himself to Moses in flaming fire on the mountain of Horeb (Exod. iii. 2, 4). With whatever veneration our first parents regarded the trees of Paradise, it appears that some which grew in natural and common earth were actually worshipped by the perverse Israelites of early ages, according to a learned Jew, one of those Rabbinical writers whose authority is most respected.*

"But the immediate object of this article and the narrow limits of an appendix do not allow me to expatiate farther amidst the groves of Scriptural history or of Jewish superstition. Nor can I enjoy more than a hasty glance at those trees reputed sacred in classical antiquity; of which such number offer themselves to the imagination as would constitute whole forests. So frequently were groves and woods dedicated to religious purposes that at last those very terms (in Greek *alsos*, *lucus* in Latin), implied consecration.

"Turning for a moment or two to the "Archæologia Græca" of the learned Dr. John Potter, we find numerous interesting items of information suitable for insertion here.

"The temples in the country were generally surrounded with groves sacred to the tutelar deity of the place, where, before the invention of temples, the gods were worshipped.

"The most usual manner of consecration of images and

---

* Moses Maimonides.

altars was by putting a crown upon them, anointing them with oil, and then offering prayers and oblations to them. Sometimes they added an execration against all that should presume to profane them, and inscribed upon them the name of the deity and the cause of their dedication. In this manner the Spartan virgins, in Theocritus's eighteenth Idyllium, promise to consecrate a tree to Helena; for it was customary to dedicate trees or plants after the same manner, and with altars and statues:

> 'We first a crown of creeping lotus twine,
> And on the shadowy plane suspend, as thine;
> We first beneath the shadowy plane distil
> From silver vase the balsam's liquid rill;
> Graved on the bark the passenger shall see
> Adore me, traveller! I am Helen's Tree.'

Ovid likewise, in the eighth book of his Metamorphoses, speaks of adorning them with ribands:

> 'An ancient oak in the dark centre stood,
> The covert's glory, and itself a wood:
> Ribands embrac'd its trunk, and from the boughs
> Hung tablets, monuments of prosperous vows.'

It may here be farther observed, that altars were often erected under the shade of trees. Thus we find the altar of Jupiter Herceus placed within the court of Priamus, king of Troy:

> 'Within the courts, beneath the naked sky,
> An altar rose; an aged laurel by;
> That o'er the hearth and household gods displayed
> A solemn gloom, a deep majestic shade.'

But where groves of trees could be had, they were preferred before any other place. It was so common to erect altars and temples in groves, and to dedicate them to religious uses, that all sacred places, even those where no trees were to be seen, were called groves, as we learn from Strabo.[*] And it seems to have been a general custom which prevailed, not only in Europe, but over all the eastern countries, to attribute a sort of religion to groves. Hence, among other precepts, whereby the Jews were kept from the imitation of

---
[*] Geograph. Lib., ix.

the Pagan religion, this was one: 'Thou shalt not plant thee a grove of any trees near unto the altar of the Lord thy God' (Deut. xvi. 21).

"This practice is thought to have been introduced into Greece from Phœnicia by Cadmus. And some are of opinion that hence Ascra, a village in Bœotia, where Hesiod was born, received its name. Several causes are assigned why groves came into so general request.

"At first, the pleasantness of such places was apt to allure the people, and to beget in them a love for the religious worship which was paid there; especially in hot countries, where nothing is more delightful and refreshing than cool shades; for which cause the sacred groves consisted of tall and beautiful trees, rather than such as yield fruit. Hence Cyril does expressly distinguish the tree fit for groves from that which bears fruit, it being the custom to plant groves, not with vines or fig trees, or others which produced fruit, but only with trees which afford no fruit for human use, merely for the sake of pleasure. Thus one of the temples of Diana is described by Herodotus as standing within a grove of the largest trees. And the way to Mercury's temple was set up on both sides with trees reaching up to heaven, as we are told by the same historian. The same is farther confirmed by the descriptions of groves which remain in the ancient poets.

"Secondly, the solitude of groves was thought very fit to create a religious awe and reverence in the minds of the people. Thus we are told by Pliny, that in groves, *ipsa silentia adoramus*, the very silence of the place becomes the object of our adoration. Seneca also observes, that when we come into such places, *illa proceritas sylvæ, et secretum loci, et admiratio umbræ, fidem numinis facit*, the height of the trees, the solitude and secrecy of the place, and the horror which the shade strikes into us, does possess us with an opinion that some deity inhabits there.

"It may not be impertinent to add one testimony more from Ovid, who speaks thus:

'A darksome grove of oak was spread out near,
Whose gloom impressive told, A God dwells here.'

"Thirdly, some are of opinion that groves derived their religion from the primitive ages of men, who lived in such places before the building of houses. Thus Tacitus reports of the ancient Germans, that they had no other defence for their infants against wild beasts or the weather than what was afforded *ramorum nexu*, by boughs of trees compacted together. All other nations lived at first in the same manner; which was derived from Paradise, the seat of the first parents of mankind. And it is not unworthy of observation, that most of the ceremonies used in religion were first taken from the customs of human life. . . .

"In latter ages, when cities began to be filled with people, and men to delight in magnificent edifices and costly ornaments, more than the country and primitive way of living, groves by degrees came into disuse. Yet such of the groves as remained from former times were still held in great veneration, and reverenced the more for the sake of their antiquity. As in the earlier times it was accounted an act of sacrilege to cut down any of the consecrated trees, which appears from the punishment inflicted by Ceres upon Erichthonius for this crime, whereof there is a prolix relation in Callimachus; so in latter ages, the same was thought a most grievous wickedness; whereof it will be sufficient to mention this one example, where Lucan speaks of Cæsar's servants, in allusion to the fable of Lycurgus, who endeavouring to destroy the vines of Bacchus, cut off his own legs:

'But valiant hands
Then falter'd. Such the reverend majesty
That wrapt the gloomy spot, they feared the axe
That struck those hallow'd trees would from the stroke
Recoil upon themselves.'—ELTON."

Ouseley proceeds—"The trunk or stump of a single tree afforded most obvious materials for a bust or statue; and even unfashioned by human art, became on some occasions an object of idolatrous worship, whilst any rude flat stone, or heap of earth at its base, served as an altar, and the surrounding grove as a temple. That groves in ancient times were considered as temples we learn from Pliny. Treating of the respect paid to trees, he says that they were formerly Temples of the Gods, and that even in his time the rustics, observing ancient usage, dedicated to the Deity any tree of pre-eminent beauty or excellence. There is authority for believing that images were placed in groves sooner than within the walls of religious edifices; also that in the formation of statues, wood was employed before stone or marble, as appears from Pausanias, and is declared by many antiquaries, as for instance Caylus, Winkelmann, and Ernesti.

"That various trees were consecrated, each to a particular divinity, we know from numerous passages so familiar to every classical reader, that I need scarcely quote on this subject Virgil and Pliny. The statue of each god was often (perhaps generally though not necessarily), made from the tree esteemed sacred to him. But I shall not here trace the idol worshipped while yet merely a rude trunk or stock, and in that state called Sanis, through the Xoanon, when the wood was pared or shaven until it became a Deikelon or Bretas, having assumed a likeness, however faint, of the human form. This progress has been described by several writers on the Religion and Arts of Greece, such as Vossius, Gronovius, Grænius and Spence, as well as those already mentioned.

"But it must not be here forgotton that as votive offerings, or as tokens of veneration, wreaths and fillets, and chaplets or garlands were often suspended from the sacred branches; a more elegant and far more innocent form of homage to a Divinity than (as among some nations) the staining of trees with blood which had just flowed from the expiring victim, not unfrequently human.

"Concerning those offerings and wreaths and chaplets, a multiplicity of Greek and Latin extracts might here be adduced, and illustrated by means of the devices on medals, and sculptured marbles, the paintings on vases, and other precious monuments of antiquity. But the limits usually assigned to an appendix admit few quotations."

Sir William proceeds to notice those lines wherein, mentioning the intended consecration of a shady plane-tree to Helen (who was daughter of Jupiter, and worshipped as a goddess in the Troad, in Rhodes and Lacedemon), Theocritus* describes the Spartan virgins declaring that they would begin the ceremony by placing on it a twisted or woven wreath of the humble growing lotus.

* Id., xviii. 43.

And Ovid's* mention of the wreaths hanging from a sacred tree, and the addition of recent offerings; and his story of Eresicthon,† who impiously violated the ancient woods of Ceres, cutting down the sacred oak, which was in itself equal to a grove, and hung round with garlands, fillets and other votive offerings.

And those lines in which Statius ‡ records a vow, promising that an hundred virgins of Calydon, who ministered at the altars, should fasten to the consecrated tree chaplets and fillets, white and purple interwoven.

And the same poet's account of the celebrated Arcadian oak, sacred to Diana, but itself adorned as a divinity, and so loaded with rustic offerings that there was "scarcely room for the branches."

The palm was deemed sacred in Egypt according to Porphyry; and Herodotus mentions those palms that surrounded the temple of Perseus (Lib. II., cap. 91); the grove of immense trees, and the trees reaching to heaven, about the temple of Bubastis or Diana (Lib. II., c. 138); and those at the great temple of Apollo (Lib. II., c. 156).

Sir William Ousley says—"We may believe, also, that a sacred mulberry tree gave its name, *Hiera Sycaminos*, to a town or station near the river Nile.

"Hiera Sycaminos, fifty-four miles above Syene, according to Pliny, Nat. Hist., Lib. VI. c. 29; also in Ptolemy's Georgr., Lib. IV., c. 5; and in the Peutingerian or Theodosian tables."

* Metam. Lib., VIII. 689.   † Metam. Lib., VIII.
‡ Theb. Lib., II. 736.

CHAPER III.

Arab Tree Worship—Story of Kaimun, the Captive Slave—Miracle of the Date Tree—Persian Bushes—Plane Tree—The Great Cypress—The Old Man of Diarbekir—The Feroüers—Anecdote of Xerxes—Anecdote of a Merchant and his Wife—The Bush of the "Excellent Tree"—The Cypresses of Zoroaster—Motawakel—The Triple Tree of Abraham—Tree of the Club of Hercules—The Tree Menelais—The Tree of Passienus Crispus—The Virgin Mary's Fig Tree—Tree of Mohammed's Staff—The Neema Tree of the Gallas—Irish Superstitions—Saint Valeri—People of Livonia—Destruction of a Sacred Tree.

AMONG the Pagan Arabs of a very early date according to Ousley, was a tree worshipped by certain tribes as an idol, under the name of *Aluzza* or *Alozza*, according to original authority, cited by the learned Pococke. This is said to have been the Egyptian Thorn or Acacia, a reference to which is found in the Preliminary Discourse to Sale's translation of the Koran. "*Al Uzza*, as some affirm, was the idol of the tribes of *Koreish* and *Kenanah*, and part of the tribe of *Salim;* others tell us it was a tree called the Egyptian Thorn or Acacia, worshipped by the tribe of Ghatsan, first consecrated by one Dhalem, who built a chapel over it called Boss, so contrived as to give a sound when any person entered."

The manuscript chronicle of Tabri, written in the ninth century, says that the people of Najrán (in Yemen or Arabia Felix) had been idolaters, like all the neighbouring tribes, until a remarkable event induced them to embrace Christianity. "And they had," says he, "outside the city, a date tree of considerable base; and every year on a certain day, they held a solemn festival; and on that day all the people assembled round the tree, and they covered it with garments of rich embroidery, and brought all their idols under it; and they went in ceremonious procession about that tree, and offered up prayers, and an evil spirit or devil spoke to them from the midst of it, and they having paid reverence to that tree, returned. It afterwards happened," continues the historian, "that a man of Syria, named Kaimun, a descendant from the Apostles of Jesus, came into Arabia, fell among thieves, was taken and sold as a slave in the land of Najrán. Here his master surprised him at midnight, reading the Gospel by a ray of celestial light, which illuminated the whole house, and Kaimun soon after, through divine assistance, caused the tree which had been worshipped as a divinity, to come forth, root and branch, from the earth; such a miracle effected an instantaneous conversion of the people, who destroyed all their idols and became zealous disciples of Jesus."

"Whatever circumstances in this anecdote may appear marvellous, there is little reason to doubt that a tree was once among the objects of idolatrous veneration at Najrán; and as we learn from authentic history, the people of that place were cruelly persecuted for their adherence to Christianity, by Dhú Nawa's, also named Yusef (Joseph), a prince of the Jewish religion, who reigned in the sixth century; about seventy years before Mahommed. That the ancient Arabians practised pagan rites, we learn from Zakaria Cazvini, who wrote in the thirteenth century. They observed, says he, at first, the religion of Abraham, but afterwards sunk into gross idolatry; some worshipping a stone, and some a tree. He then relates the story of that tree-idol, *Aluzza*, above mentioned, with a slight variation of circumstances, not claiming particular notice."

The trees and bushes which the modern Persians regard with particular respect, have been noticed by most travellers in that country. Mr. Morier, in his journey through Persia in the years 1808-9 (vol. I., p. 230), says that according to superstitious belief, the rags deposited on certain bushes by persons suffering from diseases, and taken thence by other patients, who in turn substitute their own, prove an infallible remedy. In his second volume also (p. 239), he mentions the tomb of some Persian saint, and growing close to it, a small bush on which were fastened various rags and shreds of garments; these, as was generally fancied, had acquired from their vicinity to the saint, virtues peculiarly efficacious against sickness.

In the eighteenth century, it was remarked by Chardin at Ispahan, that the religious Mahommedans chose rather to pray under a very old tree than in the neighbouring mosque. They devoutly reverence, says he, those trees which seem to have existed during many ages, piously believing that the holy men of former times had prayed and meditated under their shade.

He noticed also at Ispahan a large and ancient plane, all bristling with nails and points, and hung with rags as votive offerings from dervishes, who, like monks of the Latin church, were professed mendicants, and came under the tree to perform their devotions. He next describes another plane, said to be in his time above one thousand years old; it was black with age, and preserved with extreme care. This attention, adds he, arises from a superstitious respect entertained by the Persians for those ancient trees already mentioned. They call them *Dracte fasel*, or *the excellent trees*, venerating them as having been miraculously preserved by God so many years, because they had afforded shade and shelter to his faithful servants, the Dervishes and others professing a religious life. Another plane, one of these *excellent trees*, held in veneration, to which the devout resorted, is then described by this celebrated traveller (tome VIII., p. 187). One, also, at *Shiráz*, to which they tied chaplets, amulets, and pieces of their garments; while the sick (or some friends for them) burned incense, fastened small lighted tapers to the tree, and practised other superstitions in hopes of thereby restoring health. Throughout all Persia, adds Chardin, these *Dracte fasels* are venerated by the multitude, and they appear all stuck over with nails used in fixing in them shreds of clothes and other votive offerings. Under their shade the pious love to repose whole nights, fancying they behold resplendent lights, the souls of *Aoulia* or blessed saints, who had under the same trees performed their devotions. To those spirits, persons afflicted with tedious maladies devote themselves; and if they recover, the cure is attributed to their influence and proclaimed a miracle.

The plane trees of Persia, the reverence paid to them as divinities, and the worship accorded them on account of their great age, are mentioned also by others, notably by Father Angelo, who resided in the country for a considerable period.

Ousley says—" Pietro della Valle, in 1622, celebrated the great Cypress of Passa, anciently Pasagarda according to the general opinion; and, nearly two hundred years after, I beheld this beautiful tree with admiration equal to that expressed by the Italian traveller. He mentions that it was regarded with devotion by the Mahomedans; that tapers were often lighted in the capacious hollow of its trunk, as in a place worthy of veneration; the people respecting large and ancient trees, supposing them to be frequently the receptacles of blessed souls, and calling them on that account, *Pir* or 'aged,' a name equivalent to the Arabic *Sheikh;* also *Imám*, signifying a priest or pontiff; so they entitle those of their sect whom they imagine to have died in the odour of sanctity. Therefore when they say that such a tree or such a place is a Pir, they mean that the soul of some holy elder, a venerable personage whom they believe blessed, delights to reside in that tree or to frequent that spot. This most excellent traveller then observes that the veneration paid to trees may be considered as a remnant of ancient paganism, and aptly quotes various lines from Virgil in confirmation thereof."

Similar testimony to the above is supplied by Barbaro, who, two centuries before Chardin and Angelo, when travelling through Persia observed thornbushes to which were attached great numbers of old rags and scraps of garments, supposed to be efficacious in banishing fevers and other disorders.

"Whatever suspicion," says Ousley, "may be excited by this practice" we are discussing, "it is certain that the Mahommedans shudder at any imputation of idolatry, and fancy that in their addresses or offerings to those trees, they only invoke the true God, the great Creator. This will appear from an anecdote related by Saadi, who was born in the twelfth and lived during most part of the thirteenth century, eminent among Persian poets and philosophers. It occurs in the sixth chapter of his *Gulistan*, or Rose Garden, a work which has been published in various European languages, and so well translated into English by Mr. Gladwin, that I shall borrow his words upon this occasion, as it would be unnecessary and presumptuous to substitute my own. 'In the territory of Diarbeker I was the guest of a very rich old man, who had a handsome son.' One night he said, 'during my whole life I never had but this son. Near this place is a sacred tree, to which men resort to offer up their petitions. Many nights I besought God until he bestowed on me this son.' I heard that the son was saying to his friends in a low tone of voice, how happy should I be to know where that tree grows, in order that I might implore God for the death of my father.'"

"It seems probable that the early *Muselmans* who invaded *Iran* or Persia in the seventh century, found this invocation of trees established there from ages long elapsed, and that they soon adopted the popular superstition (if, indeed, some practices of the same or of a similar nature were not already frequent among themselves), reconciling it to their own faith, by addressing the Almighty, or, as we have seen, the intermediatory spirits of the saints. By the ancient Persians, especially those who professed Magism as reformed according to Zeratusht or Zoroaster, image-worship and other forms of gross idolatry, were held in as much abhorrence as afterwards by the Muselmans themselves; and they contemplated the Sun and its representative, material Fire, with veneration, merely as bright symbols of the sole invisible God. Yet in some of those sacred books which their descendants the *Gabrs* and Parsis attribute to Zeratusht himself (but which we may reasonably suppose were compiled in the third century, from fragments of ancient manuscripts and from tradition); it seems that trees were invoked as *pure* and *holy*, and that a form of prayer (izeshne) was particularly addressed to *Feroüers*, or spirits of saints through whose influence the trees grew up in purity, and which, placed above those trees as on a throne, were occupied in blessing them.

"From want of a more expressive term, I have called the Feroüers, 'spirits,' but it is not easy to describe by one word those imaginary creatures; for, at first, they existed singly; were then united to the beings which they represent, forming, as it would seem, part of their very souls; there are Feroüers of persons not yet born, although properly united only with rational beings, yet they are assigned to water and to trees ('Les saints Feroüers de l'eau et des arbres.'—Zendav. II., p. 284). Some are described as females; all are immortal and powerful, but beneficent; pleased with offerings, they protect their votaries, and are prompt in carrying off the petitions of those who invoke them to the mighty Ormuzd.

"Here we find the supposed agency of preternatural beings, intermediate between man and his Creator; and to this I would ascribe an act of the great Xerxes which is represented as extraordinary and even ridiculous; but of which, in my opinion, the motive has not been rightly understood.

"To Xerxes I have already alluded as the Persian king, who, almost five centuries before our era, although he may have worshipped God under the symbol of Fire or of the Sun, appears as if willing to propitiate some invisible superhuman power, by offerings suspended from the branches of a tree, in which he believed it resident.

"The anecdote is first related by Herodotus, and in such a manner as leaves but little doubt of its authenticity. The fact which it records I hope to prove conformable with Persian usage and opinion. But many circumstances are related of Xerxes by the Greek writers, which can scarcely be reconciled to probability. Xerxes, according to that venerable historian above-named, having come from Phrygia into Lydia, arrived at a place where the road branched off, leading on the left towards Caria, on the right to Sardis. Those who travel by this road, says he, must necessarily cross the river Mænder, and pass the city of Callatebos, wherein dwell confectioners, who compose sweetmeats of tamarish-honey and wheat. Xerxes, proceeding on this road found a plane tree, which on account of its beauty he decorated with golden ornaments; and leaving to guard it one of his troops, called the Immortals, advanced on the next day to Sardis, the chief city of the Lydians.

"This anecdote is related with an amplification of circumstances, and his own comments, by Ælian, who ridicules the Persian monarch because, having undertaken a very important expedition, he pitched his camp and delayed a whole day in a desert of Lydia, that he might pay homage to a great plane tree, on the branches of which he hung rich garments, bracelets, and other precious ornaments; and left a person to guard it, as if the tree had been a beloved mistress; such is the sum of Ælian's words. He does not impute this act of Xerxes (although it wore a semblance of worship) to any religious or superstitious motive, but to an absurd admiration of the tree, an inanimate object, on which from its very nature, says he, neither the gold nor splendid garments, nor the other gifts of that barbarian, could confer any benefit or additional beauty.

"To the same story Ælian alludes again, in a chapter recording instances of strange and ridiculous love; and it is noticed by Eustathius in his commentary on Homer.

"But these Greek writers could scarcely have suspected

the true motive of Xerxes in this act, since Herodotus, the very historian by whom it was first related, had described the Persian religion as incompatible with what would appear a kind of idolatry. Yet the reader has, perhaps, already seen enough to convince him that Xerxes, while he affixed his jewels and garments on the plane tree, was engaged in solemn invocation; soliciting, on the eve of an important military enterprise, the Almighty's favour through the intercession of some imaginary power.

"That such is a just interpretation of the circumstance will further appear when we consider that it is not merely in case of sickness (though a very frequent occasion), that the present Muselman Persians (no less averse from gross idolatry than their early predecessors) invoke the spirits supposed to dwell in certain trees, by hanging on the branches pieces torn from their garments; but as I have learned from several among them, on every undertaking which they deem of magnitude, such as a commercial or matrimonial speculation, the building of a new house, or a long journey; and as almost six hundred years ago, when Saadi wrote his work above quoted, offerings are daily made by votaries desirous of having children.

"On this subject an anecdote was told by a person at *Shiraz*, from whom I sought information respecting some trees and bushes covered with old rags, in the vale of *Abdui* and other places. He assured me that before the arrival of our Embassy at Bushehr, a merchant, lately married to a beautiful girl, but who had not yet given him reason to expect the blessing of an heir, was travelling with her, and finding a pleasant spot, halted there awhile, the sun's excessive heat inducing him to seek shelter. He perceived at a little distance from the road some ancient walls, among which grew a shady and handsome tree, to this he retired with his young wife, leaving the mules or horses in a servant's care. The tree, from its situation, had until that time, escaped the notice of most passengers, and did not exhibit on its branches even one votive offering, but the merchant, whose fondest wish was to obtain a son, fastened on it a shred torn from his clothes, and the united vows of himself and his fair companion were crowned with success before the expiration of a year. The circumstance being known (although some would, perhaps, think the event possible without any preternatural agency), was ascribed to the tree's efficacious influence, and within another year the branches were covered with several hundred rags, by as many votaries; not all, however, acting from the same motive."*

As might reasonably be anticipated, the imagination has readily lent itself to the development and propagation of the superstitious idea now under consideration, and we find many an ancient bush exalted into a *Dirakht-i-fazel* from the fancied appearance of fire glowing in the midst of it, and then suddenly vanishing; this name, as we have already seen, implying according to Chardin, "the excellent tree," and bestowed, as several travellers have observed, on every bough or tree that exhibits votive offerings, without regard to size or species, age, beauty or situation.

"Where trees are generally scarce, the votary," says Ousley, "must not be fastidious in selection; *Dirakht-i-fazels* are found near tombs containing the bodies of supposed saints, or Imámzádehs, but I have as frequently observed them in desert places where it could not be imagined that they derived any virtue from such sacred relics.

"As the Persian villagers in their rustic dialect give the name of *fázel* (still perhaps retaining its sense as the epithet excellent) to certain preternatural beings, so *Dirakht-i-fazel* would express 'the tree of the genii.' This circumstance I learn from a note written at my request, after some conversation on the subject, by Mirza Mohammed Saleh, of Shiraz, a very ingenious and well-informed young man of letters. And that preternatural beings were supposed to frequent a certain tree, I learn from an author of the twelfth century, quoted by Hamdallah Cozvini. He relates that among the wonders of Azerbaijan (or Media) there is at the foot of Mount *Sabalan*, a tree, about which grows much herbage; but neither is this nor the fruit of that tree ever eaten by beasts or birds, as they dislike it, and to eat of it is to die. This, as tradition reports, is the residence of jinn or genii."†

The MS. Diet of Berhan Kattea, contains a long passage concerning two cypress trees of high celebrity among the Magians, the young plants of which had been brought, it is

---

* Ousley's "Persia," vol. I.   † Ousley, vol. I.

said, from Paradise, by Zeratusht or Zoroaster himself, who in an auspicious hour planted one at *Kashmír* and the other at *Fármad*. After they had flourished one thousand four hundred and fifty years, the Arabian *Khalifah*, Motawakel (who reigned in the ninth century), commanded Taher Ben Abdallah, the governor of Khorásán, to cut them down and send both their trunks and branches to Baghdád, near which city he was constructing a palace. With such veneration were these ancient cypresses regarded by the Magians, that they offered, but in vain, fifty thousand *dinars* or pieces of gold coin, to save them from the fatal axe. At the moment of their fall, an earthquake spread consternation through the surrounding territory. Such was their immense size, that they afforded shade at once to above two thousand cows or oxen and sheep; with the branches alone, thirteen hundred camels were loaded, and in transporting the huge trunks on rollers to Baghdad, five hundred thousand *direms* (pieces of silver coin) were expended. On the very night that they reached the stage next to Motawakel's new edifice, this Khálifah was assassinated by his servants.

Ousley says—"The assassination of Motawakel happened on the tenth of December, in the year of our era 861; and not without a strong suspicion that his own son concurred in the atrocious deed."

Ancient writings supply an abundance of anecdotes relating to wonderful trees which have flourished at various periods of the world's history, but many of these are so thickly encumbered with matter purely legendary that it is often difficult to distinguish the genuine from the apochryphal.

Among others there is in a Greek manuscript preserved in the library of Augsburgh, and quoted by Jacobus Gretser, in his work "De Sancta Cruce," an account of an extraordinary triple tree, planted by the patriarch Abraham, and existing until the death of Christ—a period of about nineteen hundred years.

Greek writers tell of a wild olive which had taken root and grown from the club of Hercules, and Pausanias describes it as existing in the second century.

The same writer speaks of a number of other celebrated trees remaining in his own time, including the large and beautiful plane called *Menelais*, which was planted at Caphya by Menelaus, when engaged in military preparations for the siege of Troy, or by his brother Agamemnon, described as the "king of men," according to Pliny.

An instance of tree veneration somewhat similar to that recorded by Xerxes, already cited, may here be mentioned. According to the historian we are quoting, the consul Parsienus Crispus so loved a certain tree that he was accustomed to kiss and embrace it, to lay himself down under it and to besprinkle it with wine. "The kisses and embraces," says Ousley, "might have authorized Ælian to give the Roman consul a place in his chapter on strange and ridiculous loves. But to recline under the shade of a beautiful tree seems perfectly natural; and, perhaps, we may discover in the libation or affusion with wine, something of a religious ceremony, for it appears that the tree stood in an ancient grove consecrated to Diana, and we know that wine was sprinkled on trees in the early ages, as still in some parts of France."

Near Cairo, at a fountain wherein the Virgin Mary washed her infant's clothes, a lamp was, three centuries ago, kept burning to her honour in the hollow of an old fig tree, which had served them as a place of shelter, according to the "Itinerario de Antonio Tenreio;" and Maundrell, who travelled in 1697, saw between Jerusalem and Bethlehem, the famous turpentine tree, in the shade of which the blessed Virgin is said to have reposed when she was carrying Christ in her arms.

In the time of Hamdallah Cazvini (fourteenth century), a dry or withered tree distinguished the grave of a holy man at *Bastam;* this tree had once been (they say) Mohammed's staff, and was transmitted through many generations, until finally deposited in the grave of Abu Abdallah Dasitani, where it took root and put forth branches, like the club of Hercules. Those who injured this sacred tree perished on the same day.

In the time of Plutarch, an aged tree still bore the title of "Alexander's Oak," and marked a spot rendered memorable by one of that hero's exploits. It stood near the river Cephisus, and not far from the burial-place of many valiant Macedonians. How old this tree may have been during Alexander's youth, does not appear; but it grew near Cheronæa where he signalised himself in battle 337 years before Christ; and Plutarch died 119 years after Christ. It may, however, have existed to a much later period.

In Africa, the modern Muselmans and Pagans seem equally inclined to distinguish particular trees as sacred objects. Every tribe of the Galla nation, in Abysinnia, worship avowedly as a god, the Wanzey tree. Mr. Salt confirms this statement of Bruce, using similar language. Mungo Park mentions the Neema Tuba, a large tree decorated with innumerable rags or scraps of cloth—"a tree which nobody presumed to pass without hanging up something."

Barbot informs us that the inhabitants of Southern Guinea make offerings and pray to trees, more especially in time of sickness; from an expectation of thereby recovering their health.

Colonel Keatinge, in his "Travels in Europe and Africa," speaks of a resemblance or identity between the *Argali* (wild olive) and the *Arayel* or the sacred tree of the Hindus; and he noticed the offerings strung upon those *Argali*, "rags, potsherds, and the like trash." Why such things were offered, or the origin of such a custom, no person attempts to explain, but he observes, "a traveller will see precisely the like in the west of Ireland, and will receive an equally satisfactory account upon the subject."

A multiplicity of extracts might be quoted to prove how long this superstition lingered among various nations of Europe, besides the Irish. We need scarcely premise that it was widely diffused in pagan times throughout those nations. We have already seen it among the Greeks and Romans. It flourished among the ancient Germans, as Tacitus and Agathias inform us; among the Scandinavians also, and different tribes of the north, according to their *Edda* and other works. The Druids of the Celts, Gauls and Britons of course afford familiar examples. But after the introduction of Christianity we find the worship of trees condemned, as a practice still existing, by the councils of Auxerre, of Nantes, and of Tours. It was also strongly forbidden by the laws of Canute, as may be seen in Wilkins's "Leg. Ang. Sax."

Many anecdotes are recorded, says Ousley, of holy men who exerted themselves in efforts to abolish the superstition. Thus we read in the History of Saint Valeri, that this pious abbot, having discovered the trunk of a large tree which the rustics zealously worshipped with pagan devotion, immediately directed that it should be destroyed. Notwithstanding such laudable exertions, we learn from Ditmar, an author of the eleventh century, that in his time the people of Ridegast, in Mecklenbourgh, revered a certain gloomy forest and were afraid to touch the trees of which it was composed.

Leonard Rubenus, late in the sixteenth century, found Livonia still infected with the idolatrous veneration of trees; for passing through the sacred woods of the Esthonians, he perceived an immense pine, which the neighbouring people adored, loading its branches with pieces of old cloth, and expecting that any injury offered to it would be attended with some miraculous punishment. Rubenus, however, tells us that he cut on this pine the figure of a cross, and, lest the superstition should be thereby augmented, he afterwards marked on it the form of a gibbet, in contempt for the tree, regarded by those rustics as their god.

At a much later period this kind of idolatry existed among the same people. Abel Burja, who visited them in 1777, mentions their sacred trees, and relates an anecdote which he heard at Petersburgh from a priest of Finland, whose father had likewise exercised the sacerdotal office in that country, where his parishioners had long honoured a certain tree with religious homage. This worthy pastor, having excited the good humour of those peasants, whom he treated with brandy, exhorted them to cut down the object of their superstitious worship, but they refused to touch it, fearing that on the first application of an axe they should be destroyed by thunderbolt. Their pastor, however, struck it with impunity; encouraged by the brandy, they followed his example, and soon prostrated the ancient tree.*

* Ousley, vol. I.

CHAPTER IV.

The Bogaha of Ceylon, or God Trees—The Maha Wanse and the Bo-Tree—Ceremonies connected with the Transplantation of the Bo-Tree—Planting the Great Bo-Branch—Miracles of the Bo-Tree—The State Elephant—The Pipal Tree.

CEYLON had its *Bogaha*, or "God Tree," and when Sir William Ousley was in that country in 1810, he was presented with a number of pieces of the wood found in its forests, among the collection were samples of the *Bogaha* tree, venerated, he says, by the natives as sacred. A note from Knox's "Historical Relation of the Island of Ceylon," says—"I shall mention but one tree more, as famous and highly set by as any of the rest, if not more, though it bears no fruit, the benefit consisting chiefly in the holiness of it. This tree they call Bogauhah; we, the God Tree. It is very great and spreading; the leaves always shake like an asp. They have a great veneration for these trees, worshipping them upon a tradition that Buddou, a great god among them, when he was upon the earth, did use to sit under this kind of trees. There are many of these trees, which they plant all the land over, and have more care of than of any other. They pave round about them like a key, sweep often under them to keep them clean; they light lamps and set up their images under them, and a stone table is laid under some of them to lay their sacrifices on; they set them everywhere in towns and highways, where any convenient places are; they serve also for shade to travellers; they will also set them in memorial of persons deceased, to wit, there where their bodies were burnt. It is religion also to sweep under the Bogauhah, or God Tree, and keep it clean. It is held meritorious to plant them, which, they say, he that does shall die within a short time after and go to heaven. But the oldest men only that are nearest death in the course of nature do plant them, and none else, the younger sort desiring to live a little longer in this world before they go to the other."

The Maha Wanse, the principal native historical record

in Ceylon, supplies a great deal of interesting information respecting the sacred trees of that country, notably of the Bo-Tree. Chapter 18, as translated from the Pali by the Hon. George Turnour, is particularly important. "The ruler of the land, meditating in his own palace on the proposition of the thero, of bringing over the great Bo-Tree as well as the theri Sanghamitta; on a certain day, within the term of that 'wasso,' seated by the thero, and having consulted his ministers, he himself sent for and advised with his maternal nephew, the minister Aritho. Having selected him for that mission, the king addressed this question to him: 'My child, art thou willing, repairing to the court of Dhammasoko, to escort hither the great Bo-Tree and the theri Sanghamitta?' 'Gracious lord, I am willing to bring these from thence hither, provided on my return to this land, I am permitted to enter into the priesthood.' The monarch replying, 'Be it so,' deputed him thither. He, conforming to the injunction both of the thero and of the sovereign, respectfully took his leave. The individual so delegated, departing on the second day of the increasing moon of the month 'assayujo,' embarked at Jambokolapattana."

"Having departed, under the (divine) injunction of the thero, traversing the ocean, he reached the delightful city of Puppa on the very day of his departure.

"The princess Anula, together with five hundred virgins, and also with five hundred of the women of the palace, having conformed to the pious observances of the 'dasasil' order, clad in yellow garments, and strenuously endeavouring to attain the superior grades of the sanctification, is looking forward to the arrival of the theri to enter into the priesthood; leading a devotional life of piety in a delightful sacerdotal residence, provided (for them) by the king, in a certain quarter of the city which had previously been the domicile of the minister Dono. The residence occupied by such pious devotees has become from that circumstance, celebrated in Lanka by the name 'Upasaka.' Thus spoke Maharittho, the nephew (of Dewananpiyatisso), announcing the message of the king, as well as of the thero, to Dhammasoko; and added, 'Sovereign of elephants! the consort of thy ally the king (of Lanka), impelled by the desire of devoting herself to the ministry of Buddho, is unremittingly leading the life of a pious devotee, for the purpose of ordaining her a priestess, deputing thither the theri Sanghamitta, send also with her the right branch of the great Bo-Tree.

"He next explained to the theri herself the intent of the message of the thero (her brother Mahindo). The said theri, obtaining an audience of her father, communicated to him the message of the thero. The monarch replied (addressing her at once reverentially and affectionately), 'My mother! bereaved of thee, and separated from my children and grandchildren, what consolation will there be left wherewith to alleviate my affliction?' She rejoined, 'Maharaja, the injunction of my brother (Mahindo) is imperative; and those who are to be ordained are many; on that account it is meet that I should repair thither.'

"The king (thereupon) thus meditated—'The great Bo-Tree is rooted to the earth; it cannot be meet to lop it with any weapon: by what means then can I obtain a branch thereof?' This lord of the land, by the advice of the minister Mahadevo, having invited the priesthood to a repast, thus inquired (of the high-priest): 'Lord, is it meet to transmit (a branch of) the great Bo-Tree to Lanka?' The chief-priest, the son of Moggali, replied: 'It is fitting it should be sent;' and propounded to the monarch the five important resolves of (Buddho) the deity gifted with five means of perception. The lord of the land, hearing this reply, rejoicing thereat, ordered the road to the Bo-Tree, distant (from Pataliputto) seven yojanas, to be swept, and perfectly decorated in every respect; and for the purpose of having the vase made, collected gold. Wissakammo himself assuming the character of a jeweller, and repairing thither, enquired 'of what size shall I construct the vase?' On being told—'make it, deciding on the size thyself'—receiving the gold, he moulded it (exclusively) with his own hand, and instantly perfecting that vase, nine cubits in circumference, five cubits in depth, three cubits in diameter, eight inches in thickness, and in the rim of the mouth of the thickness of the trunk of a full-grown elephant, he departed.

"The monarch causing that vase, resplendent like the meridian sun, to be brought, attended by the four constituent hosts of his military array, and by the great body of the priesthood, which extended over five yojanas in length and three in breadth, repaired to the great Bo-Tree, which was decorated with every variety of ornament; glittering with the variegated splendour of gems; decked with rows of streaming banners; laden with offerings of flowers of every hue; and surrounded by the sound of every description of music; encircling it with this concourse of people, he screened (the Bo-Tree) with a curtain. A body of a thousand priests, with the chief thero (son of Maggali) at their head, having (by forming an inner circle) enclosed the sovereign himself as well as the great Bo-Tree most completely; with uplifted clasped hands (Dhammasako) gazed on the great Bo-Tree.

"While thus gazing (on the Bo-Tree) a portion thereof, being four cubits of the branch, remained visible, and the other branches vanished. Seeing this miracle, the ruler of the world, overjoyed, exclaimed, 'I make an offering of my empire to the great Bo-Tree.' The lord of the land (thereupon) invested the great Bo-Tree with the empire. Making flower and other offerings to the great Bo-Tree, he walked round it. Having bowed down, with uplifted hands, at eight places; and placed that precious vase on a golden chair, studded with various gems, of such a height that the branch could be easily reached, he ascended it himself for the purpose of obtaining the supreme branch. Using vermillion in a golden pencil, and therewith making a streak on the branch, he pronounced this confession of his faith. 'If this supreme right Bo branch detached from this Bo-Tree is destined to depart from hence to the land of Lanka, let it, self-severed, instantly transplant itself into the vase: then, indeed, I shall have implicit faith in the religion of Buddho.'

"The Bo branch severing itself at the place where the streak was made, hovered over the mouth of the vase (which was) filled with scented soil.

"The monarch then encircled the branch with (two) streaks above the original streak, at intervals of three inches: from the original streak, the principal, and from the other streaks, minor roots, ten from each, shooting forth and brilliant, from their freshness, descended (into the soil in the vase). The sovereign on witnessing this miracle (with uplifted hands) set up a shout, while yet standing on the golden chair, which was echoed by the surrounding spectators. The delighted priesthood expressed their joy by shouts of 'Sadhu,' and the crowding multitude, waving thousands of cloths over their heads, cheered.

"Thus this (branch of the) great Bo-Tree established itself in the fragrant soil (in the vase) with a hundred roots, filling with delight the whole attendant multitude. The stem thereof was ten cubits high: there were five branches, each four cubits long, adorned with five fruits each. From the (five main) branches many lateral branches amounting to a thousand were formed. Such was this miraculous and delightful-creating Bo-Tree.

"The instant the great Bo branch was planted in the vase, the earth quaked, and numerous miracles were performed. By the din of the separately heard sound of various musical instruments—by the 'Sadhus' shouted, as well by devos and men of the human world, as by the host of devos and brahmas of the heavens—by the howling of the elements, the roar of animals, the screeches of birds, and the yells of the yakkhas, as well as other fierce spirits, together with the crashing concussions of the earthquake, they constituted an universal chaotic uproar.

"From the fruits and leaves of the Bo branch, brilliant rays of the six primitive colours issuing forth, illuminated the whole 'chakkawalan.' Then the great Bo branch, together with its vase, springing up into the air (from the golden chair), remained invisible for seven days in the snowy regions of the skies.

"The monarch descending from the chair, and tarrying on that spot for those seven days, unremittingly kept up in the fullest formality, a festival of offerings to the Bo branch. At the termination of the seventh day, the spirits which preside over elements (dispelling the snowy clouds), the beams of the moon enveloped the great Bo branch.

"The enchanting great Bo branch, together with the vase, remaining poised in the firmament, displayed itself to the whole multitude. Having astounded the congregation by the performance of many miracles, the great Bo branch descended to the earth.

"The great monarch, overjoyed at these various miracles, a second time made an offering of the empire to the great Bo. Having thus invested the great Bo with the whole empire, making innumerable offerings, he tarried there for seven days longer.

"On the fifteenth being the full moon day of the bright half of the month assayujo (the king) took possession of the great Bo branch. At the end of two weeks from that date, being the fourteenth day of the dark half of the month assayujo, the lord of chariots, having had his capital fully ornamented and a superb hall built, placing the great Bo branch in a chariot, on that very day brought it in a procession of offering (to the capital).

"On the first day of the bright half of the month 'Kattiko,' having deposited the great Bo branch under the great Sal tree in the south-east quarter (of Patilaputto) he daily made innumerable offerings thereunto.

"On the seventeenth day after he had received charge of it, its new leaves sprouted forth simultaneously. From that circumstance also the monarch, overjoyed, a third time dedicated the empire to the great Bo-Tree.

"The ruler of men, having thus finally invested the great Bo branch with the whole empire, made various offerings to the said tree.

"The lord of chariots assigned for the custody of the Bo branch, eighteen personages of royal blood, eighteen members of noble families, eight of the Brahman caste, and eight of the Settha caste. In like manner eight of each of the agricultural and domestic castes, as well as of weavers and potters, and of all other castes: as also Nagas and Yakkos. This delight in donations, bestowing vases of gold and silver, eight of each (to water the Bo branch with), embarking the great Bo branch in a superbly decorated vessel on the river (Ganges), and embarking likewise the high-priestess Sanghamitta with her eleven priestesses, and the ambassador, Arittho at the head (of his mission); (the monarch) departing out of his capital, and preceding (the river procession with his army) through the wilderness of Winjha, reached Tamalitta on the seventh day. The devas and men (during his land progress) kept up splendid festivals of offerings (on the river), and also reached (the port of embarkation) on the seventh day.

"The sovereign disembarking the Bo branch on the shore of the main ocean, again made an offering of his empire. This delighter of good works having thus finally invested the great Bo branch with the whole empire, on the first day of the bright half of the moon in the month of

'Maggasiro;' thereupon he (gave direction) that the great Bo branch which was deposited (at the foot of the Sal tree) should be lifted up by the aforesaid four high caste tribes (assisted) by the other eight persons of each of the other castes. The elevation of the Bo branch having been effected by their means (the monarch) himself descending there (unto the sea) till the water reached his neck, most carefully deposited it in the vessel.

"Having thus completed the embarkation of it, as well as of the chief theri with her priestesses, and the illustrious ambassador Maharittho, he made this address to them:— 'I have on three occasions dedicated my empire to this great Bo branch; in like manner let my ally, your sovereign, as fully make (to it) an investiture of his empire.'

"The maharaja, having thus spoken, stood on the shore of the ocean with uplifted hands; and gazing on the departing Bo branch, shed tears in the bitterness of his grief. In the agony of parting with the Bo branch, the disconsolate Dhammasoko, weeping and lamenting in loud sobs, departed for his own capital.

"The vessel in which the Bo-Tree was embarked, briskly dashed through the water; and in the great ocean, within the circumference of a yojana, the waves were stilled: flowers of the five different colours blossomed around it, and various melodies of music rung in the air. Innumerable offerings were kept up by innumerable devas; (but) the nagas had recourse to their magical arts to obtain possession of the Bo-Tree. The chief-priestess, Sanghammitta, who had attained the sanctification of 'abhinna,' assuming the form of the 'supanna,' terrified those nagas (from their purpose). These subdued nagas, respectfully imploring of the chief-priestess (with her consent) conveyed the Bo-Tree to the settlement of the nagas: and for seven days innumerable offerings having been made by the naga king, they themselves, bringing it back, replaced it in the vessel. On the same day that the Bo-Tree reached this land at the port of Jambukolo, the universally beloved monarch Dewananpiyatisso, having by his communications with Sumano Samanero, ascertained the (approaching) advent (of the Bo branch); and from the first day of the month of 'maggasiro,' in his anxiety to prepare for its reception, having, with the greatest zeal, applied himself to the decoration of the high road from the northern gate (of Anuradhapura) to Jambukolo, had (already) repaired thither.

"While seated in a hall on the sea-beach, by the miraculous powers of the thero (Mahindo), he was enabled to discern (though still out of sight) the Bo branch which was approaching over the great ocean. In order that the hall built on that spot might perpetuate the fame of that miracle, it became celebrated there by the name of the 'Sammudasanna-sala.' Under the auspices of the chief thero, attended by the other theros, as well as the imperial array of his kingdom, on that very day, the nobly formed maharaja, chanting forth in his zeal and fervour, 'This is the Bo from the Bo-Tree (at which Buddho attained buddhohood),' rushing into the waves up to his neck, and causing the great Bo branch to be lifted up collectively by the sixteen castes of persons on their heads, and lowering it down, deposited it in the superb hall built on the beach. The sovereign of Lanka invested it with the kingdom of Lanka; and unto these sixteen castes, surrendering his sovereign authority, this ruler of men, taking upon himself the office of sentinel at the gate (of the hall), for three entire days in the discharge of this duty, made innumerable offerings.

"On the tenth day of the month, elevating and placing the Bo branch in a superb car, this sovereign, who had by inquiry ascertained the consecrated places, exhorting the monarch of the forest, deposited it at the Pachina wiharo; and entertained the priesthood as well as the people, with their morning meal. There (at the spot visited at Buddha's second advent) the chief thero Mahindo narrated, without the slightest omission, to his monarch, the triumph obtained over the nagas (during the voyage of the Bo branch) by the deity gifted with the ten powers. Having ascertained from the thero the particular spots on which the divine teacher had rested or taken refreshment, those several spots he marked with monuments.

"The sovereign stopping the progress of the Bo branch at the entrance of the village of the Brahma Tiwako, as well as at the several aforesaid places, (each of which) was sprinkled with white sand, and decorated with every variety of flowers, with the road (approaching to each) lined with banners and garlands of flowers:—and keeping up offerings, by night and by day uninteruptedly, on the fourteenth day he conducted it to the vicinity of Anuradhapura. At the hour that shadows are most extended, he entered the superbly decorated capital by the northern gate, in the act of making offerings; and passing in procession out of the southern gate, and entering the Mahamego garden hallowed by the presence of the Buddhas (of this kappo); and arriving under the directions of Sumano himself, at the delightful and decorated spot at which the former Bo-Trees had been planted;—by means of the sixteen princes who were adorned with all the insignia of royalty (which they assumed on the king surrendering the sovereignity to them), raising up the Bo branch, he contributed his personal exertion to deposit it there.

"The instant it extricated itself from the hand of man, springing eighty cubits up into the air, self poised and resplendent, it cast forth a halo of rays of six colours. These enchanting rays illuminating the land, ascended to the Brahma heavens, and continued (visible) till the setting of the sun. Ten thousand men, stimulated by the sight of these miracles, increasing in santification, and attaining the state of 'arabat,' consequently entered into the priesthood.

"Afterwards, at the setting of the sun, the Bo branch descending, under the constellation 'rohani,' placed itself on the ground, and the earth thereupon quaked. Those roots (before described) rising up out of the mouth of the vase, and shooting downwards, descended (forcing down) the vase itself into the ground. The whole assembled populace made flower and other offerings to the planted Bo. A heavy deluge of rain fell around, dense cold clouds completely enveloped the great Bo in its snowy womb. In seven days the Bo-Tree remained there, invisible in the snowy womb, occasioning (renewed) delight in the populace. At the termination of the seventh day, all these clouds dispersed, and displayed the Bo Tree, and its halo of six coloured rays.

"The chief thero Mahindo and Sanghmitta, each together with their retinue, as well as his majesty with his suite, assembled there. The princes from Chandanaggamo, the Brahma, Tiwako, as also the whole population of the land, by the interposition of the devas, exerting themselves to perform a great festival of offerings (in honour) of the Bo Tree, assembled there; and at this great congregation, they were astounded at the miracles which were performed.

"On the south-eastern branch a fruit manifested itself, and ripened in the utmost perfection. The thero taking up that fruit as it fell, gave it to the king to plant it. The monarch planted it in a golden vase, filled with odoriferous soil, which was prepared by the Mohasano. While they were all still gazing at it, eight sprouting shoots were produced, and became vigorous plants four cubits high each. The king, seeing these vigorous Bo-Trees, delighted with astonishment, made an offering of, and invested them with, his white canopy (of sovereignty).

"Of these eight he planted (one) at Jambukolopatana, on the spot where the Bo-Tree was deposited on its disembarkation; one at the village of the Brahma Tiwako; at the Thuporamo; at the Issarasamanako wiharo; at the Pattama Chetiyo; likewise at the Chetiyo mountain wiharo; and at Kachharagoms, as also at Chandanagamo (both villages in the Rohona division); one Bo plant at each. These bearing four fruits, two each, (produced) thirty Bo plants, which planted themselves at the several places, each distant a yojano in circumference from the sovereign Bo-Tree, by the providential interposition of the supreme Buddha, for the spiritual happiness of the inhabitants of the land.

"The aforesaid Anula, together with her retinue of five hundred virgins, and five hundred women of the palace, entering into the order of priesthood in the community of the theri Sanghamitta, attained the sanctification of 'arahat.' Arittho, together with a retinue of five hundred personages of royal extraction, obtaining priestly ordination in the fraternity of the also thero, attained 'arahat.' Whoever the eight persons of the setti caste were who escorted the Bo-Tree hither, they, from that circumstance, obtained the name of bhodahara (bo-bearers).

"The theri Sanghamitta together with her community of priestesses sojourned in the quarter of the priestesses, which obtained the name of the 'Upasaka wiharo.'

"There at the residence of Anula, before she entered into the priesthood (the king) formed twelve apartments, three of which were the principal ones. In one of these great apartments (called the Chulangono) he deposited the (Kupayatthikan) mast of the vessel which transported the great Bo; in another (called Mahaangano) an oar (piyam); in the third (called the Siriwaddho, the arittan) rudder. From these (appurtenances of the ship) these (appartments) were known (as the Kupayatthitapanagara).

"Even during the various schisms (which prevailed at subsequent periods) the Hatthalaka priestess uninterruptedly maintained their position at the establishment of twelve apartments. The before-mentioned state elephant of the king, roaming at his will, placed himself at a cool stream in a certain quarter of the city, in a grove of kadambo-trees, and remained browsing there: ascertaining the preference given by the elephant to the spot, they gave it the name of 'Hattalakan.'

"On a certain day this elephant refused his food; the king enquired the cause thereof of the thero, the dispenser of happiness in the land. The chief thero, replying to the monarch, thus spoke: '(the elephant) is desirous that the thupo should be built in the kadambo grove.' The sovereign, who always gratified the desires of his subjects, without loss of time built there a thupo, enshrining a relic therein, and built an edifice over the thupo.

"The chief theri, Sanghamitta, being desirous of leading a life of devotional seclusion, and the situation of her sacerdotal residence not being sufficiently retired for the advancement of the cause of religion and for the spiritual comfort of the priestesses, she was seeking another nunnery. Actuated by these pious motives, repairing to the aforesaid delightful and charmingly secluded thupo edifice, this personage sanctified in mind and exalted by her doctrinal knowledge, enjoyed there the rest of noonday.

"The king repaired to the temple of the priestesses to pay his respects to the theri, and learning whither she had gone, he also proceeded thither, and reverentially bowed down to her. The maharaja Dewananpiyatisso, who could distinctly divine the thoughts of others, having graciously consulted her, inquired the object of her coming there, and having fully ascertained her wishes, erected around the thupo a charming residence for the priestesses. This nunnery being constructed near the Hatthalaka hall, hence became known as the 'Hatthalaka wiharo.' The chief theri Sanghamitta, surnamed Sumitta, from her being the benefactress of the world, endowed with divine wisdom, sojourned there in that delightful residence of priestesses.

"Thus, this (Bo-Tree) monarch of the forest, endowed with miraculous powers, has stood for ages in the delightful Mahamego garden in the Linka, promoting the spiritual welfare of the inhabitants of Lanka, and the propagation of the true religion."

No trees, perhaps, are held in greater veneration in India, than the *Ficus Religiosa* or pipal tree. It is known as Rarvasit, the tree of knowledge and wisdom, the holy "Bo-Tree" of the lamas of Thibet. Balfour's "Indian Cyclopædia" says —"This large handsome tree grows in most of the countries of Asia, and is frequently to be met with near pagodas, houses and other buildings. One at Gyaine, South Behar, is said to have been that beneath which Sakya was reposing when his views as to his duties became clear to him, and if so, is more than 2,400 years old. It is also held in veneration by the Hindus, because the god Vishnu is fabled to have been born under its branches. In the Somavati festival, the Mahratta women circumambulate a pipal tree, and place offerings on it, when the new moon falls on a Monday. The pipal tree is preferable for avenues to the banyan. The leaves are heart-shaped, long, pointed, wavy at the edge, not unlike those of some poplars, and as the footstalks are long and slender, the leaves vibrate in the air like those of the aspen tree. Silkworms prefer the leaves next to those of the mulberry. The roots are destructive to buildings, for if once they establish themselves among the crevices, there is no getting rid of them."

"It is the most sacred of trees with the Buddhists, who say it was under this tree that Gautama slept, and dreamed that his bed was the whole earth, and the Himalaya mountains his pillow, while his left arm reached to the Eastern Ocean, his right to the Western Ocean, and his feet to the great South Sea. This dream he interpreted to mean that he would soon become a Buddha. A branch of the tree was sent to Ceylon in the year 250 B.C., by Asoka—to the city of Amūrādhapōora—together with certain relics of Gautama: his collar-bone, begging-dish, &c.; and it flourishes there as the Bo-Tree. For upwards of twenty centuries it had been an object of the profoundest veneration to the people, and particularly to the pilgrims in their annual visits to the ruins of the city."

Fergusson says—"Whatever may be the result of the investigation into the Serpent Worship of Ceylon, there is no doubt whatever about the prevalence and importance of Tree Worship in that island. The legend of the planting of the Râjâyatana Tree by Buddha has already been alluded to, but the history of the transference of a branch of the Bo-Tree, from Buddh-gaya to Anurâdnapury, is as authentic and as important as any event recorded in the Ceylonese annals. Sent by Asóka (250 B.C.), it was received with the utmost reverence by Devanampiyatisso, and planted in a most conspicuous spot in the centre of his capital. There it has been reverenced as the most important 'numen' of Ceylon for more than 2,000 years, and it, or its lineal descendant, sprung at least from the old root, is there worshipped at this hour. The city is in ruins; its great dagobas have fallen to decay; its monasteries have disappeared; but the great Bo-Tree still flourishes according to the legend—'Ever green, never growing or decreasing, but still living on for ever for the delight and worship of mankind.' Annually thousands repair to the sacred precincts within which it stands, to do it honour, and to offer up those prayers for health and prosperity which they believe are more likely to be answered if uttered in its presence. There is probably no older idol in the world, certainly none more venerated."

Stories illustrating the peculiar reverence with which this tree is regarded are tolerably plentiful, and but for the limitations of our space, might be almost indefinitely multiplied. A writer in *Notes and Queries* relates that an old woman in the neighbourhood of Benares, was observed walking round and round a certain peepul-tree. At every round she sprinkled a few drops of water from the water vessel in her hand on the small offering of flowers she had laid beneath the tree. A bystander who was questioned as to this ceremony, replied—"This is a sacred tree; the good spirits live up amidst its branches, and the old woman is worshipping them."

Then some half-a-dozen years ago, when Mr. Barnum, the showman, of America, was completing the purchase of a certain white elephant, it was narrated in an Indian paper, that under the terms of sale, the purchaser was required to swear by the holy and sacred Bo-Tree that the animal should receive every kindness and consideration.

CHAPTER V.

Sacred Trees very ancient in Egypt—Hebrew Trees—The Sycamore at Matarea—Ionic forms—The Koran on Mary and the Palm Tree—Sacredness of the Palm in Egypt—Tree Worship in Dahome—The sacred tree of the Canary Isles.

"AMONG the Egyptians, from the earliest period of their monumental history to the latest, we find represented on tombs and stèts the figure of a sacred tree, from which departed souls in human form, receive the nourishment of everlasting life.

"The monuments of the ancient Assyrians also show a sacred tree symbolical of the divine influence of the lifegiving deity. So also do those of the ancient Persians, and it was preserved by them, almost as represented on the Assyrian monuments, until the invasion of the Arabs.

"The Hebrews had a sacred tree which figured in their temple architecture along with the cherubim; it was the same sort of tree as that which had previously been in use among the Egyptians, and was subsequently, in a conventional form, adopted by the Assyrians and Persians, and eventually by the Christians, who introduced it in the mosaics of their early churches associated with their most sacred rites. This tree, which occurs also as a religious symbol on Etruscan remains, and was abbreviated by the Greeks into a familiar ornament of their temple architecture, was the date palm, *Phœnix dactylifera.*

"But although the earliest known form of the Tree of Life on Egyptian monuments is the date palm, at a later period the sycamore fig tree was represented instead, and eventually even this disappeared in some instances and a female personification came in its place.

"Besides the monumental evidence thus furnished of a sacred tree, a Tree of Life, there is historical and traditional evidence of the same thing, found in the early literature of various nations, in their customs and popular usages."*

* Barlow's Symbolism.

The sycamore at Matarea in Egypt is still shown, which miraculously opened ionically to receive and reproduce the persecuted virgin when avoiding the cruelty of Herod.

Moor, the author of "Oriental Fragments," while noting that it does not appear that the sycamore was especially a mystical tree among any ancient people, and that he does not see anything mystical or peculiar in it, says:— "but here may be traced another link connecting through distant countries the chain of mystery in this line of thought—that is, of the mysticism of clefts or ionic forms and transit and trees. Those beautiful and interesting objects of producing and reproducing nature connect themselves, in the mystic contemplative eye, with all that is beautiful and interesting, and poetical and profound. They point up to the heavens, they strike down to Tartarus, but are still of earth:—a Brahmanal triad expressed by the Sanscrit word *bhurbhuvaswah*—heaven, earth, sky—a vastly profound trisyllabic-mono-verbal-mythos; holding, like the mighty Aum, or Om, in mystic combination, the elementals of Brahma, Vishnu and Siva."

The commendable delicacy, generally speaking of Mohammedans, and the prosaic nature of their religion, forbid sexual allusions in their writings, and without impugning their fastidiousness on that point—not indeed always observable even in the *Koran*—we find there, and in the commentaries, a connection of birth and tree not very unlike what has been told or shadowed respecting Juno Samia, or Latona, and the Hindu Samia.

In the nineteenth *Sura* or chapter of the *Koran* entitled "Mary," much concerning the miraculous conception occurs. Having praised St. John, as a "devout person, and dutiful towards his parents; not proud or rebellious," and invoked a blessing on him in these words: "Peace be on him, the day whereon he was born, and the day whereon he shall die, and the day whereon he shall be raised to life;" the prophet continues: "And remember the story of Mary when the pains of child-birth came upon her near the trunk of a palm tree." "A withered trunk," adds a commentator, "without any head or verdure; notwithstanding which, though in the winter season, it miraculously supplied her with fruits for her nourishment." "And he who was beneath her," continues the Koran, "called to her saying, shake the palm tree, and it shall let fall ripe dates upon thee ready gathered."

Commentators differ as to whether it was the infant or the angel Gabriel who so called to the mother. They say "the dry trunk revived and shot forth green leaves, and a head laden with ripe fruit."

The note in Sale's translation says: "It has been observed that the Mohammedan account of the delivery of the Virgin Mary very much resembles that of Latona, as described by the poets, not only in this circumstance of their laying hold on a palm-tree (though some say Latona embraced an olive-tree, or an olive and a palm, or else two laurels), but also in that of their infants speaking."

Amongst the trees held sacred in Egypt, the palm ranked highest; and for this reason, that species of tree was most frequently used in the sacred buildings of that country, as indeed they afterwards were in those of the Hebrews, not perhaps for the same cause: for that was connected with the Sabian idolatries, which the latter were taught to detest. The real source of the veneration of the former for palm trees, and of the general cultivation of that plant in Egypt, which abounded with noble groves of them, is alleged to have been the following: They thought the palm tree, which is affirmed by Porphyry to bud every month in the year, a most striking emblem of the moon, from whose twelve annual revolutions those months are formed. Whether or not there be any truth in this, it is not easy to say, but it has been remarked by Pococke, that many of the most ancient pillars in the Egyptian temples bear great resemblance to palm trees, and that their capitals are made in imitation of the top of that tree when all the lower branches are cut off; and possibly, he adds, the palm trees said to be cut in Solomon's temple, might be only pillars, or at least pilastres of this kind. In his plate of Egyptian pillars may be seen various columns of this description, and a very remarkable one belonging to the temple of Carnack. Several of the capitals also in other plates bear an evident similitude to the expanded top of trees with their branching foliage cut off or compressed.

Captain Burton in his "Mission to Gelele," says: "In

the days of Bosman (1700) the little kingdom of Whydah adored three orders of gods, each presiding, like the several officers of a prince, over its peculiar province.

"The first is the Danh-gbwe, whose worship has been described. This earthly serpent is esteemed the supreme bliss and general good; it has 1000 Danh'si or snake-wives, married and single votaries, and its influence cannot be meddled with by the two following which are subject to it.

"The second is represented by lofty and beautiful trees, 'in the formation of which Dame Nature seems to have expressed her greatest art.' They are prayed to and presented with offerings in times of sickness, and especially of fever. Those most revered are the Hun-'tin, or acauthaceous silk cotton (Bombax), whose wives equal those of the snake, and the Loko, the well-known Edum, ordeal or poison tree of the West African coast. The latter numbers few Loko-'si, or Loko spouses; on the other hand, it has its own fetish pottery, which may be bought in every market. An inverted pipkin full of cullender holes is placed upon the ground at the tree foot, and by its side is a narrow-necked little pot into which the water offering is poured. The two are sometimes separated by a cresset shaped fetish iron, planted in the earth. The *cultus arborum*, I need hardly say, is an old and far-spread worship; it may easily be understood as the expression of man's gratitude and admiration. The sacred trees of the Hindu were the Pippala (*Ficus religiosa*), the Kushtha (*Cortus speciosus*), the sacred juice of the Soma, which became a personage, and many others. The Jews and after them the early Christians and the Moslems, had their Tuba or Tree of Paradise. Mr. Palgrave, traversing Arabia in 1862—63, found in the kingdom of Shower or Hail distinct tree worship, the acacia (*Talh*) being danced round and prayed to for rain. In Egypt and other Moslem lands rags and cloths are suspended to branches, vestiges of ancient Paganism. North European mythology embraced Yggdrasit, or the World Tree. We no longer approach the gods with branches of this sacred vegetation in hand; still the maypole and Christmas tree, the yule log and the church decorations of evergreens, holly and palms, and the modern use of the sterility-curing mistletoe, descend directly from the *treovve-ordung*, or tree-worship of ancient England."

Captain George Glass, in his "History of the Canary Islands," chapter 13, on the island of Hierro, says:—On account of the scarcity of water, the sheep, goats and swine here do not drink in the summer, but are taught to dig up the roots of fern and chew them to quench their thirst. The great cattle are watered at the fountains, and at a place where water distils from the leaves of a tree. Many writers have made mention of this famous tree; some in such a manner as to make it appear miraculous; others again deny the existence of any such tree, among whom is Father Feyjoo, a modern Spanish author, in his "Theatro Critico." But he, and those who agree with him in this matter, are as much mistaken as they who would make it appear to be miraculous. This is the only island of all the Canaries which I have not been in; but I have sailed with natives of Hierro, who when questioned about the existence of this tree, answered in the affirmative."

The author of the History of the Discovery and Conquest has given us a particular account of it, which I shall relate here at large.

"The district in which this tree stands is called Tigulahe, near to which, and in the cliff or steep rocky ascent that surrounds the whole island, is a narrow gutter or gulley, which commences at the sea and continues to the summit of the cliff, where it joins or coincides with a valley, which is terminated by the steep front of a rock. On the top of this rock grows a tree, called in the language of the ancient inhabitants, Garse, *i.e.* Sacred or Holy Tree, which for many years has been preserved sound, entire and fresh. Its leaves constantly distil such a quantity of water as is sufficient to furnish drink to every living creature in Hierro; nature having provided this remedy for the drought of the island. It is situated about a league and a half from the sea. Nobody knows of what species it is, only that it is called Til. It is distinct from other trees and stands by itself; the circumference of the trunk is about twelve spans, the diameter four, and in height from the ground to the top of the highest branch forty spans: the circumference of all the branches together is one hundred and twenty feet. Its fruit resembles the acorn and tastes something like the kernal of the pine apple, but is softer and more aromatic. The leaves of this tree resemble those of the laurel, but are larger, wider, and more curved; they come forth in a perpetual succession, so that the tree is always green. On the north side of the trunk are two large tanks or cisterns of rough stone, or rather one cistern divided, each half being twenty feet square, and sixteen spans in depth. One of these contains water for the drinking of the inhabitants, and the other that which they use for their cattle, washing and suchlike purposes.

"Every morning near this part of the island a cloud or mist arises from the sea, which the south and easterly winds force against the fore-mentioned steep cliff, so that the cloud having no vent but by the gutter, gradually ascends it and from thence advances slowly to the extremity of the valley, where it is stopped and checked by the front of the rock which terminates the valley, and then rests upon the thick leaves and wide-spreading branches of the tree, from whence it distils in drops during the remainder of the day, until it is at length exhausted, in the same manner that we see water drip from the leaves of trees after a heavy shower of rain. This distillation is not peculiar to the garse or til, for the bresos, which grow near it, likewise drop water; but their leaves being but few and narrow, the quantity is so trifling, that though the natives save some of it, yet they make little or no account of any but what distils from the til; which together with the water of some fountains and what is saved in the winter season, is sufficient to serve them and their flocks. This tree yields most water in those years when the Levant or easterly winds have prevailed for a continuance; for by these winds only, the clouds or mists are drawn hither from the sea. A person lives on the spot near which this tree grows who is appointed by the council to take care of it and its water, and is allowed a house to live in, with a certain salary. He every day distributes to each family of the district seven pots or vessels full of water, besides what he gives to the principal people of the island."

CHAPTER VI.

Usefulness of the Ash Tree—Its position among Sacred Trees—The Queen of Trees—Mythology of the Ash—Scotch superstitious usages—The "Ash Faggot Ball" Somersetshire—Pliny and others on the Serpent and the Ash—The Ash as a medim of cure of complaints—Anecdotes—Phallic Associations—The New Birth—Ireland and the Ash—The Juniper Tree—The Madonna and the Juniper—The Elm Tree—Mythology of the Elm—The Apple Tree—Mythological allusions to the Apple Tree—The Pine Tree—Wind Spirits—German Superstitions—The Oak Tree—Universal Sacredness of the Oak—The Oak of the Hebrew Scriptures—Classic Oaks—Socrates and his oath—Greek sayings—The Trees speaking—Sacred Oak of Dodona—Legend of Philemon and Baucis—The Hamadryads—The Yule Log—St. Boniface—Mysteries connected with the Oak—The Christmas Tree.

THE Ash, while one of the most useful and valuable of British trees, demands particular attention from the fact that it has always held a foremost position amongst the sacred trees of ancient nations. In the Scandinavian mythology it was the mundane tree—the symbolical tree of universal life. "Best and greatest of trees," it was called, "with a triple root reaching to the mythic regions of the first giants and the Æsir, and penetrating to the nebulous Niflheim, its majestic stem overtopping the heavens, its branches filling the world; it is sprinkled with the purest water, whence comes the dew that falls on the dales, its life-giving energy is diffused throughout all nature."

It has been said that if the oak be regarded as the king of trees and the Hercules of the forest, the ash may fairly claim supremacy as their queen, and Gilpin terms it the "Venus of the Woods."

"At its foot is the Undar fountain where sit the three Norns or Fates—time past, time present, and time to come; these give Runic characters and laws to men, and fix their destinies. Here is the most holy of all places, where the gods assemble daily in council, with All-Father at their head.

"These three Norns have a certain analogy to the three mythic Persian destinies seated by the fountain of perennial life; and the tree itself is evidently a symbol of that inscrutable power which is the life of all things; thus representing, under an arborescent form, the most ancient theory of nature, analogous to that personified in the Indian *Parvati*, the goddess of life and reproduction; also in the Egyptian *Isis*; and in the figure so frequently met with in the museums of Italy, called 'Diana of the Ephesians,' a variety of the Indian *Maya*.

"In the Chinese sacred books, 'the *Taou* (the divine reason or wisdom, but here put for the *Deity*) preserves the heavens and supports the earth: he is so high as not to be reached, so deep as not to be followed, so immense as to contain the whole universe, and yet he penetrates into the minutest things.' The sacred ash of the Scandinavians corresponds as a symbol with the Chinese *Taou*."*

Hesiod and Homer both mention the ash; the latter mentioning the ashen spear of Achilles, and telling us that it was by an ashen spear that he was slain.

In the heathen mythology, Cupid is said to have made his arrows first of ash wood, though they were afterwards formed of cypress.

So much mystery has always been associated with the ash tree, that in all ages and in all countries innumerable superstitions have grown up in connection with it, and, from their modern propagation in an age of education, will evidently die hard.

In many parts of the Highlands of Scotland, at the birth of a child, the nurse puts one end of a green stick of this tree into the fire, and while it is burning gathers in a spoon the sap or juice which oozes out at the other end, and administers it as the first spoonful of food to the newly-born babe.

In Somersetshire, and some other counties, the burning of an ashen fagot is a regular Christmas custom, and it is supposed that misfortune will certainly fall upon the house where it is not duly fulfilled. In the same county, there is held annually the "Ash Faggot Ball." The fagot is bound with three withes, which are severally chosen to

---

* Barlowe's "Symbolism."

represent them by the young people present—the first withe that breaks in the fire signifying that they who selected it will be the first to be married. It is said that these customs prevail extensively where the Arthurian legends are very strong, and that "it is probable that the association of the ash with Arthur grew out of its dedication to the gods of war, on account of toughness for weapons."

While many of the surviving superstitions connected with the ash may probably be traced to Yggdrasill, it has been observed that though Yggdrasill was an ash, there is reason to think that, through the influence of traditions, other sacred trees blended with it. Thus while the ash bears no fruit, the Eddas describe the stars as the fruit of Yggdrasill. "This" says Mr. Conway, "with the fact that the serpent is coiled around its root, and the name Midgard, *i.e.*, midst of the garden, suggest that the apple-tree of Eden, may have been grafted on the great ash." He also says there is a chapel at Coblentz where a tree is pictured with several of the distinctive symbols of Yggsdrasill, while on it the forbidden fruit is represented partly open, disclosing a death's head. The serpent is coiled round the tree's foot. When Christian ideas prevailed, and the Norse deities were transformed to witches, the ash was supposed to be their favourite tree. From it they plucked branches on which to ride through the air. In Oldenburg it is said the ash appears without its red buds on St. John's Day, because the witches eat them on the night before, on their way to the orgies of Walpurgisnacht.

Froschmäuster along with Pliny records the ancient popular belief that a serpent will rather pass through fire in endeavouring to escape from an enclosed circle than go under the shade of or touch the bough of the ash. In connection with this, Dioscorides affirms that the juice of ash leaves, mixed with wine, is a cure for the bite of serpents.

Another and a studiedly cruel superstition was that if a hole were bored in an ash tree and a live shrew mouse enclosed therein and left to perish, a few strokes with a branch of the tree thus prepared would cure lameness and cramp in cattle, afflictions supposed to have been brought on by the influence of the same little animal.

In our first volume of Phallic Worship an interesting

reference was made to certain curative properties supposed to be connected with the passing of a diseased or afflicted body through a cleft stick, twig, or tree.

Just here, when writing upon the ash tree, it is proper again to allude to that peculiar custom, or superstition. This tree was long held in great veneration even in our own country for its supposed virtue in removing rickets or healing internal ruptures. Newspapers and old magazines record many instances illustrative of the profound faith of many of the country folk in this mode of getting relief, and the method of procedure appears to have been nearly always the same, and akin to the passing of a diseased or polluted person through a human image in the eastern parts of the world.

The author of the "Natural History of Selborne" says that in Hampshire a tree was chosen, young and flexible, and its stem being severed longitudinally, the fissure was kept wide open, and the child to be healed, being duly undressed, was passed three times through the aperture. After the operation, the tree was bandaged up and plastered over with loam. It was believed that if the severed parts of the tree united the child and the tree gradually recovered together; if the cleft continued to gape, which could only happen through neglience or want of skill, it was thought that the operation had proved ineffectual.

Another account in a newspaper forty years ago says a poor woman applied to a farmer residing in the same parish for permission to pass a sick child through one of his ash trees. The object was to cure the child of the rickets. The mode in which the operation was performed was as follows:—A young tree was split from the top to about the height of a person, and laid sufficiently open to pass the child through. The ceremony took place before three o'clock in the morning, and before the sun rose. The child had its clothes removed. It was then passed through the tree by the woman and received on the other side by some person. This was done three times and on three consecutive mornings; the ash was then carefully bound together.

In the *Gentleman's Magazine* for June, 1804, a letter from a correspondent says: "On Shorley Heath, Warwickshire, on the left-hand side of the road going from Shorley Street to Hockley House, there stands a young ash tree, close to the cottage of Henry Rowe, whose infant son, Thomas Rowe, was drawn through the trunk or body of it, in the year 1791, to cure him of a rupture, the tree being split open for the purpose of passing the child through it. The boy is now thirteen years and six months old. I have this day, June 19th, 1804, seen the ash tree and Thomas Rowe, as well as his father Henry Rowe, from whom I received the above account; and he superstitiously believes that his son Thomas was cured of the rupture by being drawn through the cleft in the said ash tree, and by nothing else."

In the month of October following, another correspondent says: "The ash-tree described by your correspondent grows by the side of Shirley Street, at the edge of Shirley Heath, in Solihull parish. The upper part of the gap formed by the chisel has closed, but the lower part remains open, and the tree is healthy and flourishing. Thomas Chillingworth, son of the owner of an adjoining farm, now about thirty-four, was when an infant about a year old passed through a similar tree—now perfectly sound—which he preserves with so much care that he will not suffer a single branch to be touched, for it is believed that the life of the patient depends on the life of the tree, and the moment that it is cut down, be the patient ever so distant, the rupture returns, and mortification ensues and terminates in death, as was the case in a man driving a waggon on the very road in question. Rowe's son was passed through the present tree in 1722, at the age of one or two. It is not, however, uncommon for persons to survive for a time the felling of the tree. In one case the rupture returned suddenly and mortification followed. These trees are left to close of themselves or are closed with nails. The wood-cutters very frequently meet with the latter. One felled on Bunman's farm was found full of nails. This belief is so prevalent in this part of the country, that instances of trees that have been employed as a cure are very common. The like notions obtain credit in some parts of Essex."

With regard to the choice of a particular tree for these superstitious cures, Moor says: "The ash is said to be the tree always selected on these occasions, perhaps because it is more easily cleft than most others, and may more readily recover of such a wound. I have heard of a bramble being substituted, but not on ocular authority."

There is no passage in the Christian or Hebrew Scriptures on which, as concerning the ash, the Talmudists or Targumists could in such proneness build anything mysterious. The ash is but once—Isa xliv. 14—mentioned in the Bible, and this is in a plain non-mystical manner.

It may here be observed that the ash was of old a venerated tree. Hesiod makes it the origin of his brazen men. Among the mysteries of the Scandinavians, the whole human race is of the same origin. From one species of ash the Calabrians gather manna. It exudes in summer from incisions or perforations, which almost necessarily assume, when made and when healed an Ionic form. Another species of ash is poisonous: again connecting it with Sivaic or Kalaic fable. The mountain ash, a tree differing generically, I believe, from the common ash, shares also in the mysterious repute. In days of greater superstition than the present, it was used as a counterspell against witchcraft. If its name of mountain ash has been given to it from its supposed love of elevated regions, it will become more and more connected with Kali, in her character of the "mountain-born, mountain-loving Diana;" who, in one of her characters, corresponds with the obstetric Lucina."

A scholar, duly imbued with mysticism, might, haply, trace and connect sundry poetical and widely-spread superstitious allusions to the ash. Moor says: "Only one peculiarity in it occurs to me; this is, that the wood of young ash is as tough, hard, and durable as of old: of seven years as of seventy. This, with a certain class might seem a type or symbol of youth and age. In common with the sycamore, the ash tree bears, and is propagated, by a key, as we and certain other nations call the seed." In our volume on Phallism, in the chapter on the *Crux Ansata* we have seen something of the mysticism connected with that name and form, and it is not necessary to repeat it here. Moor says: "It might be insufferable to hint at the Kalaic sound in the initial of *Clauis*: and that possibly something astronomical may have been fancied in the configuration of the spots on the singularly disposed black peculiarity of the foliage of the sycamore; such leaves moreover in their exterior form being triunical and bifurcated at their base."

"A longitudinal wound in the bark of a tree will

primarily assume the Sivaic form—the erect, obeliscal! like the tree itself, symbolic of the *Linga*. Expanded, for a mysterious purpose—and it is curious what a number of such mysterious purposes seem to have occurred to prurient eyes—it is Ionic. Duplicated, when healing and healed, we find it still of like allusion."

Moor proceeds: "In rural wanderings I have been struck with the uniformities of the wounds in trees—all, be they recent or healed, incisions or perforations, in sound or hollow trees, exhibiting that almost all-pervading form so mystical in the eye of a Saiva, or a Sakti, or an Ioni jah; and perhaps of Brahmans generally. As such they are borne on the foreheads of Hindus of the present day, as they were of old; and as they probably were also among the Egyptians; and, more of individual or official than sectarial distinction perhaps among the Israelites.

With Hindus, in a word, it is the form of nature's matrix; with Plutonists, or Vulcanists, or Saiva, it is creation—it is heat—it is renovation—it is fire—it is regeneration—it is all in all. So it is with Neptunists, the Vaishnavas: then, of course, of aqueous, in lieu of igneous, reference. "What is the sea," they say, "but the hollow of the hand—the great *argha*—of nature—or matrice of production and reproduction?"

"In the seemingly whimsical operation of the cleft tree, now more immediately under our notice, the all-pervading form and feeling may be recognised. A child issuing head first (by some practitioners feet first) through such cleft—or a man through a natural or artificial similar fissure or cleft in a rock, or through a like form of metal, down to the ridiculous cut cheese of Oxford—all seem to be indications of obstetricity, and would not fail of reminding a 'twiceborn' Brahman of a 'second birth' or regeneration — of which mysterious matter his ceremonial and spiritual books abound.

The 'new birth' of Christians—let it not be deemed irreverent to mix such subjects—is expressly declared and universally understood to be of grace; spiritual, though it produce no visible fruits. Superstition, the offspring of ignorance and craft, may occasionally symbolize it into carnality. But such is the proneness of Brahmans to general sexualization that although their esoteric dogma of regeneration is said to be sufficiently guarded on that point, it has notwithstanding, from such proneness, been degraded into doctrines and ritual ceremonies that we may term mythological, or whimsical, or ridiculous, or worse.

"The investiture of the 'twice-born'—a common periphrasis for a Brahman—of a mystical triple cord, or rather a thread diversely re-triplicated up to the number ninety-six, is understood to be a purifying rite. This thread has several names. That by which it is mostly called is *Zennaar*. By western writers it has been common to call it the "sacerdotal thread,' or the ' Brahminical thread,' meaning thereby, probably, to confine it to priests. But it is not confined to priests nor to Brahmans. The two next classes wear it and are canonically and ceremonially entitled. If the reader supposes that Brahman and priest are synonymous he is in error. With Hindus all priests are Brahmans. Through this mystical *zennaar*, or *vinculum*, the sanctified person is passed with endless ceremonials. The figurative language common in eastern idioms of 'twice born,' being 'made whole' &c., is with us spirituality. But it is by others misunderstood, and hence those who are not 'broken-hearted,' not 'broken in spirit,' but broken in body, seek to be 'made whole' by a physical rite ; and pass regeneratively through a *zennaar*, or a tree, or a stone, of a peculiar form or figure." *

In Ireland the mountain ash, according to a popular belief, was an antidote to charms, and a protective against witchcraft, the evil-eye and disease. In Scotland, known as the rowan-tree or roun-tree, it was similarly regarded, a branch of it being placed over the door of the cowshed for the safely of the cattle. The saying was :

"Rowan tree and red thread
Put the witches to their speed."

Its position in Scandinavian mythology we mention at length in other pages.

Pliny says such is its influence that snakes will not rest in its shadow, shunning it at a distance. From personal knowledge, he says if a serpent be so encompassed by a fence of ash leaves as that he cannot escape without passing through fire, he will prefer the fire rather than come in contact with the leaves.†

* Oriental Fragments.   † Lib. xv., c. 24

"The juniper," says De Gubernatis, "is much venerated in Italy, in Germany, and on the shores of the Baltic, by reason of its alleged power to dispel evil influences. In Esthonias, holes and crevices in the walls or dwellings are beaten with a branch of juniper, lest evil spirits bring sickness there. When the wicked spirits draw nigh and see the juniper they take themselves off. At Pistoja the explanation given of a local custom of hanging a branch of juniper over every door is that whenever witches see the juniper they are impelled by an uncontrollable desire to count the leaflets; but these are so numerous that they can never make the number right, and in despair take flight lest they be surprised and detected. There is an analogous belief in Germany. In Waldeck, according to Dr. Maunhardt, when a child falls sick it is customary for the parents to put a lock of wool and a piece of bread in a bunch of juniper, that the evil spirits may find employment in eating and spinning therein, and so forget the child, with whom it is feared, they have been over busy.

> 'Ye fiends and ministers of hell
> Here bring I wherewithal that ye may spin,
> And eat likewise;
> Eat, therefore, and spin,
> And forget my child.'"*

In Germany a "Frau Wachholder" (Dame Jupiter) personifies the genius of the juniper tree, and is invoked to make robbers give up their spoil. A branch of a juniper bush is bent down to the ground and kept down with a stone, the name of the real or supposed thief being repeated at the same time, with injunctions to bring back the booty. Whenever the desired result comes about the stone is removed and the branch set free. Here seems to be a counterpart of the thief-catching staff or rod of Indian folk-lore, which survives in so many Aryan usages and customs. Like other trees with hispid foliage, the juniper has the special attribute of detaining fugitives; but it sometimes shields them as well. An Italian legend described the Madonna as saved in her flight by a juniper bush, just as in German story the holy Walpurga is hidden from her pursuers by a peasant in a patch of wheat. An

* Le Mythologie des Plantes, vol. II.

aged crone of Signa, in Tuscany, thus relates the legend to De Gubernatis:—Our Lady was flying with the infant Jesus, and Herod's soldiers were in hot pursuit. As they went the broom trees and chick peas rustled, risking betrayal; the flax stood bolt upright and apart; but as the fugitives drew near, a juniper bush parted its branches to receive them in its friendly embrace. Wherefore the Virgin then and there cursed both the broom and the chick pea, which from that day forth have never ceased to rustle. The fragility of the flax she forgave, but she laid her blessing on the juniper; and to this day at Christmastide, in nearly every Italian stall juniper is hung, as bunches of holly are in England, France, and Switzerland."

"Like the holly, juniper drives away evil influences of every kind from house and fold, and is held to be peculiarly efficacious in protecting horses and cattle from the incorporeal monsters which sometimes haunt and trouble them.

"In a very rare little work, published at Bologna in 1621, the author, Amadeo Castra, makes mention of a Bolognese custom on Christmas Eve of distributing branches of juniper to every house. He adds, that all writers are agreed as to its efficacy against serpents and venomous beasts; that it supplied the wood of the cross; that it covered the flight of Elias; finally arriving at the conclusion that the sanctity of the juniper equals that of the cedar; that its usage is not a fashion or superstition, but a holy mystery; and that as its fragrant smoke arises from our hearths we should remember that so should our prayers ascend to the ears of the Deity."*

"The ancients regarded the Elm as a funereal tree, it is said, because it bears not fruit; but De Gubernatis supposes because of its longevity and the ease with which it multiplies.

"In Catullus, the elm is the husband and the vine the wife. So, too, the Sanscrit Kâlidasa makes the mango the husband of a climbing plant, a species of jasmine. When the charming Sakuntala comes into the presence of the young king Dushyanti, one of the female courtiers murmurs in the king's ear, 'This *navamallika* (jasmine) that you

* "Forestry Journal," vol. VIII.

call the light of the forest is married of her own free will to *sahakara* (the mango).'

"In the 'Iliad,' Achilles bridges the enchanted streams Xanthus and Simois with the trunks of an elm tree. When Achilles kills the father of Andromache he raised in his honour a tomb, around which the nymphs came to plant elms. At the first note of Orpheus' lyre bewailing the loss of Eurydice, there sprang up a forest of elms."*

"The Apple tree was formerly supposed to be the Tree of Knowledge, the fruit of which was eaten by Eve in Paradise; and it is a curious fact, that the apple tree is also distinguished by legends in the mythologies of the Greeks, the Scandinavians, and the Druids. The pagans believed that the golden fruit of the Hesperides, which it was one of the labours of Hercules to procure, in spite of the fierce dragon that guarded them and never slept, were apples; though modern writers have supposed them oranges. In the *Edda*, we are told that the goddess Iduna had the care of apples which had the power of conferring immortality; and which were consequently reserved for the gods, who ate of them when they began to feel themselves growing old. The evil spirit Loke took away Iduna and her apple tree, and hid them in a forest where they could not be found by the gods. In consequence of this malicious theft, everything went wrong in the world. The gods became old and infirm; and, enfeebled both in body and mind, no longer paid the same attention to the affairs of the earth; and men having no one to look after them, fell into evil courses, and became the prey of the evil spirit. At length, the gods finding matters get worse every day, roused their last remains of vigour, and, combining together, forced Loke to restore the tree.

"Hercules was worshipped by the Thebans, under the name of Melius, and apples were offered at his altars. The origin of this custom was the circumstance of the river Asopus having on one occasion overflowed its banks to such an extent, as to render it impossible to bring a sheep across it which was to be sacrificed to Hercules; when some youths, recollecting that an apple bore the same name as a sheep in Greek, offered an apple, with four little sticks

* "Forestry," p. 132.

stuck in it to resemble legs, as a substitute for the sheep; and after that period the pagans always considered the apple as specially devoted to Hercules."*

The Pine tree, from a very early date, has been by many races looked upon as sacred. It was consecrated in Greece to Poseidon and Dionysius, and as sacred to Zeus was beloved by the Virgins. In the pastorals of Longus, Chloe is adorned with a *Pinea Corona* as an emblem of virginity, which Daphne takes from her and puts on her own head.

"Diana, or maids mix its chaplets with the mastic, as a tree of all others most fruitful, but not with the myrtle, which, as sacred to Venus, may not appear in a professed virgin's wreath." (Forlong.)

The position occupied by the tree in Assyria may be seen in Mr. Layard's works, he speaks of it as the "sacred tree" along with the "corner stone." "The corner stone," says Forlong, "is usually considered the principal stone of a building, hence the *principle* in each religion is called its principal or corner stone, and the fruit of this most sacred tree is the commonest and best gift to the gods. This is probably why we find the tree everywhere, and why the Assyrian priests are usually shown as presenting a pine cone to their gods and altars. The seed cone seems, however, to be at times the cone of Indian corn, but Mr. Layard thinks that the pine or cypress cone is most used in the 'Cult de Venus.' The Thyrsus of Bacchus, we may remember, has a fir cone, and the Bacchic Pole is usually held to be of pine, as very inflammable and odoriferous—it is remarkably like the insignia of Boodhism and of most other faiths, as the Tri-Sool or three thorns of Siva, the tridents of Neptune, and other deities."

The pine was supposed by some to be inhabited by wind spirits, like Ariel, owing to the whispering noise proceeding from it in the breeze. The legend was that it was the mistress of Boreas and Pan, an idea acceptable to the German mind in consequence of its holes and knots, which were believed to be the means of ingress and egress for the spirits. It is told that a beautiful woman of Småland, who was really an elf, left her family through a knot-hole

---

* Landon's "Arboretum."

in the wooden house-wall. "Frau Fichte," the pine of Silesia, is believed to possess great healing powers, and its boughs are carried about by the children on Mid-Lent Sunday, adorned with coloured papers and spangles; it is also carried with songs and rejoicing to the doors of stables where it is suspended in the belief that it will preserve the animals from harm.

In other parts superstitions equally striking prevail. In Bohemia men think if they eat the kernel of the pine cone from the top of a tree on St. John's Day they will be invulnerable against shot. A writer in "Fraser's Magazine" in 1870, said that he saw sprigs of pine stuck on the railway wagons bearing the German soldiers into France. In some parts of Germany it is quite common for a man subject to gout to climb a pine tree and tie a knot in its highest shoot as a cure for his malady, saying as he does it: "Pine, I bind here the gout that plagues me."

With many nations of antiquity the oak tree was regarded as a special object of religious veneration, such as the Kelts, the Teutonic races, the Druids, the early inhabitants of Palestine, the early Greeks and Hebrews.

Between the Hebrew customs and those of the Druids a very marked resemblance has been traced by various writers of learning and ability. In ancient Jewish history the oak is often mentioned and in a manner which seems to ascribe to it a symbolical meaning. According to Kitto "it was regarded as the emblem of a divine covenant, and indicated the religious appropriation of any stone monument erected beneath it; it was also symbolical of the divine presence, possibly from association."*

From the earliest ages the oak has been considered as one of the most important of forest trees. Held sacred alike by Hebrews, Greeks, Romans, Gauls and Britons, "it was the fear of the superstitious for their oracle and at the same time the resort of the hungry for their food." Early history is full of references to this tree. In Genesis xii., 6, 7, mention is made of the plain of Moreh, where it is said God appeared to Abram, the proper rendering of the word plain being oak. The plain of Mamre also occurs, and wherever it does should be oak or ash groves. Genesis

---

* Barlow.

xviii., 1, for instance, where it is recorded that the angels announced to the patriarch the birth of Isaac. This oak, Jewish tradition says was, long after Abraham's time, held as an object of veneration, indeed Bayle in his "Historical and Critical Dictionary," article "Abraham," says:—"This puts me in mind of the oak of Mamre, under which Abraham is said sometimes to have cooled himself. This oak, they tell you, was standing in the reign of Constantine." Loudon mentions that this tree or rather the grove of Mamre, is frequently alluded to in the Old Testament; and in Eusebius's "Life of Constantine" we find the oaks of Mamre expressly mentioned as a place where idolatry was committed by the Israelites, close to the tomb of Abraham, and where Constantine afterwards built a church. Numerous other instances may be found of the mention of the oak in the Scripture not necessary to enter into here.

Turning to classic lore, the references are even more numerous. We have the oak groves of Dodona, in Epirus, the most ancient and celebrated of oracles, whose priests sent out their revelations on its leaves.

Pliny says that the oaks in the forest of Hereynia were believed to be as old as the world, also that oaks existed at the tomb of Ilus near Troy, which had been sown when that city was first called Ilium.

Socrates took oath by the oak; also the women of Priene, a maritime city of Ionia, in matters of importance. On Mount Lycæus, in Arcadia, there was a temple of Jupiter with a fountain, into which the priest threw an oak branch, in times of drought, to produce rain. The Greeks had two remarkable sayings relative to this tree, one of which was the phrase: "I speak to the oak," as a solemn asseveration; and the other, "born of an oak," applied to a foundling; because anciently children, when the parents were unable to provide for them, were frequently exposed in the hollow of an oak tree.

So important a position does the oak occupy in the history of the subject we are now discussing, that before dismissing it we feel bound to call attention to some of those mythological allusions to it which have been collected by Loudon for the enrichment of the pages of his admirable "History of the Trees and Shrubs of Britain."

"The oak was dedicated by the ancients to Jupiter, because it was said that an oak tree sheltered that god at his birth on Mount Lycæus, in Arcadia; and there is scarcely a Greek or Latin poet or prose author, who does not make some allusion to this tree. Herodotus first mentions the sacred forest of Dodona (ii. c. 57.) and relates the traditions he heard respecting it from the priests of Egypt. Two black doves, he says, took their flight from the city of Thebes, one of which flew to the temple of Jupiter Ammon and the other to Dodona, where, with a human voice, it acquainted the inhabitants that Jupiter had consecrated the ground, which would in future give oracles. All the trees in the grove became endowed with the gift of prophecy; and the sacred oaks not only spoke and delivered oracles while in a living state, but, when some of them were cut down to build the ship 'Argo,' the beams and masts of that ship frequently spoke and warned the Argonauts of approaching calamities. (See Hom. Ody., xiv.; Lucian, vi., 427; Apoll., Book I., &c.) After giving the account above related, Herodotus adds what he calls the explanation of it. He says that some Phœnician merchants carried off an Egyptian priestess from Thebes into Greece, where she took up her residence in the forest of Dodona, and erected there, at the foot of an old oak, a small temple in honour of Jupiter, whose priestess she had been at Thebes. The town and temple of Dodona are said by others to have been built by Deucalion immediately after the great flood, when, in gratitude for his preservation, he raised a temple to Jupiter, and consecrated the oak grove to his honour. This grove, or rather forest, extended from Dodona to Chaonia, a mountainous district of Epirus, so called from Chaon, son of Priam, who was accidently killed there by his brother Helenus. The forest was, from this, sometimes called the Chaonian Forest; and Jupiter Chaonian Father. (See Virgil, Ovid, &c.) The oracle of Dodona was not only the most celebrated but the richest in Greece, from the offerings made by those who came to it, to enquire into futurity. The prophecies were first delivered by doves which were always kept in the temple, in memory of the fabulous origin assigned to the oracle; but afterwards the answers were delivered by the priestesses; or, according to Suidas, Homer and others, by the oaks themselves: hollow trees no doubt being chosen, in which a priest might conceal himself. During the Thracian war a deputation of Bœotians consulting the oracle, the priestess told them that "if they would meet with success, they must be guilty of an impious action:' when in order to fulfil the oracle, they seized her and burnt her alive. After this the Dodonian oracles were always delivered to the Bœotians by men. The oracular powers of the Dodonian oaks are frequently alluded to, not only by the Greek and Latin poets, but by those of modern times. (See Cowper's Address to the Yardley Oak and Wordsworth's Lines to a Spanish Oak.)

"Milo of Croton was a celebrated athlete, whose strength and voracity were so great that it was said he could carry a bullock on his shoulders, kill it with a blow of his fist, and afterwards eat it up in one day. In his old age, Milo attempted to tear up an old oak tree by the roots; but the trunk split and the cleft part uniting, his hands became locked in the body of the tree; and being unable to extricate himself, he was devoured by wild beasts. (Ovid; Strab; Paus.)

"The oak was considered by the ancients as the emblem of hospitality; because when Jupiter and Mercury were travelling in disguise, and arrived at the cottage of Philemon, who was afterwards changed into an oak tree, they were treated with the greatest kindness. Philemon was a poor old man who lived with his wife Baucis in Phrygia, in a miserable cottage, which Jupiter, to reward his hospitality, changed into a magnificient temple, of which he made the old couple priest and priestess, granting them the only request they made to him, viz., to be permitted to die together. Accordingly, when both were grown so old as to wish for death, Jove turned Baucis into a lime tree, and Philemon into an oak; the two trees entwining their branches, and shading for more than a century the magnificent portal of the Phrygian temple.

"The civic crown of the Romans was formed of oak; and it was granted for eminent civil services rendered to the state, the greatest of which was considered to be the saving of the life of a Roman citizen.

"Acorns having been the food of man till Ceres introduced corn, boughs of oak were carried in the Eleusinian mysteries.

"Boughs of oak with acorns were carried in marriage ceremonies, as emblems of fecundity. Sophocles, in the fragment of Rhizotomi, describes Hecates as crowned with oak leaves and serpents. Pliny relates of the oaks on the shores of the Cauchian Sea, that, undermined by the waves and propelled by the winds, they tore off with them vast masses of earth on their interwoven roots, and occasioned the greatest terror to the Romans, whose fleets encountered these floating islands. Of the Hyrcynian forest he says, "These enormous oaks, unaffected by ages and coeval with the world by a destiny almost immortal, exceed all wonder. Omitting other circumstances that might not gain belief, it is well known that hills are raised up by the encounter of the jostling roots; or where the earth may not have followed, that arches, struggling with each other, and elevated to the very branches, are curved as it were into wide gateways, able to admit the passage of whole troops of horse."

"This forest is described by Cæsar as requiring sixty days to traverse it; and the remains of it are supposed by some to constitute the forest on the mountains of the Hartz; and by others to be the Black Forest of the Tyrol.

The beautiful fiction of the Hamadryads is frequently referred to by the Greek poets. The Hamadryads were nymphs, each of whom was

'Doomed to a life coeval with her oak.'

Callimachus, in the Hymn to Delos, represents Melia as "sighing deeply for her parent oak;" and adds—

'Joy fills her breast when showers refresh the spray:
Sadly she grieves when autumn's leaves decay.'

"In Appollonius Rhodius, Book II., we find one of the Hamadryads imploring a woodman to spare the oak to which her existence is attached:

"Loud through the air resounds the woodman's stroke,
When lo! a voice breaks from the groaning oak.
'Spare, spare my life! a trembling virgin spare!
Oh, listen to the Hamadryad's prayer!
No longer let that fearful axe resound;
Preserve the tree to which my life is bound!
See from the bark my blood in torrents flows,
I faint, I sink, I perish from your blows.'"

"The oak, evidently, was an object of worship among the Celts and ancient Britons. The Celts worshipped their

God Teut under the form of this tree; and the Britons regarded it as a symbol of their God Tarnawa, the god of thunder."

Just here we are reminded by Loudon and others of the Yule log and Yule festival, a most ancient British institution, now known to our dwellers in towns only by historical report. Professor Burnet tells us the word yule comes from Hu, the Bacchus of the Druids; others derive it from Baal, Bal, or Yiaoul, the Celtic god of fire, and who was sometimes identified with the sun and worshipped under the form of an oak. Baal was considered the same as the Roman Saturn, and his festival (that of Yule) was kept at Christmas, which was the time of the Saturnalia. The Druids professed to maintain perpetual fire; and once every year all the fires belonging to the people were extinguished, and relighted from the sacred fire of the Druids. This was the origin of the Yule log, with which, even so lately as the commencement of the last century, the Christmas fire in some parts of the country was always kindled; a fresh log being thrown on and lighted, but taken off before it was consumed, and reserved to kindle the Christmas fire of the following year. The Yule log was always of oak; and as the ancient Britons considered that it was essential for their hearth fires to be renewed every year from the sacred fire of the Druids, so their descendants thought that some misfortune would befall them if any accident happened to the Yule log. (See Irving's "Bracebridge Hall.")

The worship of the Druids was generally performed under an oak; and a heap of stones was erected on which the sacred fire was kindled, which was called a cairn, as Professor Burnet says, from Kern an acorn.

The well-known chorus of "Hey derry down," according to this gentleman, was a druidic chant, signifying, literally, "In a circle the oaks move round."

Criminals were tried under an oak tree; the judge being placed under the tree, with the jury beside him, and the culprit placed in a circle made by the chief Druid's wand. The Saxons also held their national meetings under an oak, and the celebrated conference between the Saxons and the Britons, after the invasion of the former, was held under the oaks of Dartmoor.

The wood of the oak was appropriated to the most memorable uses: King Arthur's round table was made of it, as was the cradle of Edward III., who was born at Carnarvon Castle; this sacred wood being chosen in the hope of conciliating the feelings of the Welsh, who still retained the prejudices of their ancestors, the ancient Britons.

It was considered unlucky to cut down any celebrated tree; and Evelyn gravely relates a story of two men who cut down the Vicar's Oak, in Surrey; one losing his eye and the other breaking his leg soon after. (See Loudon's Arb. et Frut. Brit.)

The reverence with which the oak was regarded was by no means confined to the Celts. St. Boniface during his wanderings in Central Germany waged a sharp war against the heathen superstitions connected with trees and wells. There was a Thor's Oak (the oak was in an especial manner dedicated to Thor) of enormous size in the country of the Hessians, greatly reverenced by the people, which, following the advice of some of the Christian converts, St. Boniface determined to cut down. Accordingly he began to hew at the gigantic trunk, whilst the heathen folk stood round about, prodigal of their curses, but not daring to interfere. The tree had not been half cut through, when, says Willibrord, the biographer of Boniface, who was himself present, a supernatural wind shook the great crown of its branches, and it fell with a mighty crash divided into four equal parts. The heathens, he continues, recognised the miracle, and most of them were converted on the spot. With the wood of the fallen tree St. Boniface built an oratory, which he dedicated in honour of St. Peter.*

The destruction of this oak has been considered a wise step, as it was evidently a matter of tremendous difficulty, in spite of innumerable decrees and canons condemnatory of heathen ceremonies in connection with trees, to get rid of the idolatry while the object of it remained.

Sometimes the tree was, as it is called, re-appropriated by the saint of the district; then the evils resulting seemed as bad as ever. There was St. Colman's oak, for instance, any fragment of which, kept in the mouth, was

---

* Life by Willibrord, chap. viii.

believed would effectually ward off death by hanging. There was also St. Columba's oak at Kenmare which, when blown down in a storm, no one dared to touch, or to apply the wood of it to ordinary purposes, except a certain tanner, who used the bark for curing leather. With the leather he made himself a pair of shoes; but the first time he put them on he was struck with leprosy, and remained a leper all his life.

It has for ages, in England, been thought that the oak was specially and mysteriously protected. Aubrey in his history of Surrey says:—"A strange noise proceeds from a falling oak, so loud as to be heard at half-a-mile distant, as if it were the genius of the oak lamenting. It has not been unusually observed that to cut oak-wood is unfortunate. There was at Norwood one oak that had mistletoe, a timber tree, which was felled about 1657. Some persons cut this mistletoe for some apothecaries in London, and sold them a quantity for ten shillings each time, and left only one branch remaining for more to sprout out. One fell lame shortly after; soon after each of the others lost an eye; and he that felled the tree, though warned of these misfortunes of the other men, would, notwithstanding, adventure to do it, and shortly after broke his leg; as if the Hamadryades had resolved to take an ample revenge for the injury done to their venerable oak. I cannot here omit taking notice of the great misfortunes in the family of the Earl of Winchelsea, who, at Eastwell in Kent, felled down a most curious grove of oaks, near his own noble seat, and gave the first blow with his own hands. Shortly after his countess died in her bed suddenly; and his eldest son, the Lord Maidstone, was killed at sea by a cannon bullet."

Grimm points out many superstitions connected with the oak in Germany. It is believed in India that holes in trees are doors through which the special spirits of those trees pass, and this is found in Germany in the idea that the holes in the oaks are pathways for elves; and that certain troubles, especially of hand or foot, may be cured by contact with these holes. Near Gundalskol stood an oak popularly regarded as the habitation of a "Bjarmand," but he was driven away by the church bells. It is said that a farmer was engaged to an elf-girl, but instead of a bride he embraced an oak sapling. In a churchyard at Heddinge, Seeland, are the remains of an oak wood declared to be the soldiers of the Erl-King, assuming the forms of armed men at night. In Westphalia, it is the custom to announce formally to the nearest oak any death that has occurred in a family. The process of healing rupture, once common in England, with the ash, is performed in Germany with the oak.

"The Christmas-tree has become a prevailing fashion in England at this season, and is by most persons supposed to be derived from Germany; such however is not the fact; the Christmas-tree is from Egypt, and its origin dates from a period long antecedent to the Christian era. The palm-tree is known to put forth a shoot every month, and a spray of this tree, with twelve shoots on it, was used in Egypt at the time of the winter solstice, as a symbol of the year completed. Egyptian associations of a very early date still mingle with the tradition and custom of the Christmas-tree; there are as many pyramids as trees used in Germany, in the celebration of Christmas, by those whose means do not admit of their purchasing trees and their concomitant tapers. These pyramids consist of slight erections of slips of wood, arranged like a pyramidal *epergne*, covered with green paper, and decorated with festoons of paper-chain work, which flutters in the wind and constitutes a make-believe foliage. This latter, however, is an innovation of modern days."*

* Willis's Current Notes for February, 1854.

CHAPTER VII.

Icelandic customs—The Sacred Ash—The Prose Edda and Tree Worship—Icelandic Mythology of the Ash—The Norns—The Czeremissa of the Wolga—The Jakuhti—Sacred Trees of Livonia—Phallic Tree Worship and objects in Bavaria.

IN his "Northern Antiquities," M. Mallet says: "We have seen that the Icelandic mythology reckons up twelve goddesses, including Frigga, the spouse of Odin, and the chief of them all. Their names and respective functions will be found in the Prose Edda. Besides these twelve goddesses there are numerous virgins in Valhalla, or the paradise of the heroes. Their business is to wait upon them and they are called Valkyrior. Odin also employs them to choose in battles those who are to perish, and to make the victory incline to whatever side he pleases. The court of the gods is ordinarily kept under a great ash tree and there they distribute justice. This ash is the greatest of all trees; its branches cover the surface of the earth, its top reaches to the highest heaven, it is supported by three vast roots, one of which extends to the ninth world. An eagle, whose piercing eye discovers all things, perches upon its branches. A squirrel is continually running up and down it to bring news; while a parcel of serpents, fastened to the trunk, endeavour to destroy him. From under one of the roots runs a fountain wherein wisdom lies concealed. From a neighbouring spring (the fountain of past things) three virgins are continually drawing a precious water, with which they water the ash tree: this water keeps up the beauty of its foliage, and, after having refreshed its leaves, falls back again to the earth, where it forms the dew of which the bees make their honey. These three virgins always keep under the ash, and it is they who dispense the days and ages of men."

"In the 'Prose Edda' just alluded to, a piece of ancient Norse literature commonly ascribed to Snorri Sturluson, we get a good deal respecting the veneration and regard paid by the people to this tree.

"'Where,' asked Gangler, 'is the chief or holiest seat of the gods?'

TREE WORSHIP.

"'It is under the ash Yggdrasill,' replied Har, 'where the gods assemble every day in council.'

"'What is there remarkable in regard to that place?' said Gangler.

"'That ash,' answered Jafnhar, 'is the greatest and best of all trees. Its branches spread over the whole world, and even reach above heaven. It has three roots very wide asunder. One of them extends to the Æsir, another to the Frost-giants in that very place where was formerly Ginnungagap, and the third stands over Niflheim, and under this root, which is constantly gnawed by Nidhögg, is Huergelmir. But under the root that stretches out towards the Frost-giants there is Mimir's Well, in which wisdom and wit lie hidden. The owner of this well is called Mirmir. He is full of wisdom, because he drinks the waters of the well from the horn Gjoll every morning. One day All-Father came and begged a draught of this water, which he obtained, but was obliged to leave one of his eyes as a pledge for it. As it is said in the Völuspá—

> 'All know I, Odin!
> How thou hiddest thine eye
> In Mimir's well-spring
> Of limpid water.
> Mead quaffs Mimir
> Each morn from the pledge
> Valfadir left him.
> Conceive ye this or not?'

"'The third root of the ash is in heaven, and under it is the holy Urdar-fount. 'Tis here that the gods sit in judgment. Every day they ride up hither on horseback over Bifröst, which is called the Æsir Bridge. These are the names of the horses of the Æsir: Sleipner is the best of them; he has eight legs and belongs to Odin. The others are Gladyr, Gyllir, Glær, Skeidbrimir, Silfrintoppr, Synir, Gils, Falhöfnir, Gulltoppr and Lettfeti. Baldur's horse was burnt with his master's body. As for Thor, he goes on foot, and is obliged every day to wade the rivers called Körmt and Œrmt, and two others called Kérlaung.'

"'Through these shall Thor wade every day, as he fares to the doomstead under Yggdrasill's ash, else the Æsir Bridge would be in flames and boiling hot would become the holy waters.'

"'But tell me,' said Gangler, 'does fire burn over Bifröst?'

"'That,' replied Har, 'which thou seest red in the bow, is burning fire; for the Frost-giants and the Mountain-giants would go up to heaven by that bridge if it were easy for everyone to walk over it. There are in heaven many goodly homesteads, and none without a celestial ward. Near the fountain, which is under the ash, stands a very beauteous dwelling, out of which go three maidens, named Und, Verdaudi, and Skuld. These maidens fix the life-time of all men and are called Norns. But there are indeed many other Norns, for when a man is born there is a Norn to determine his fate. Some are known to be of heavenly origin, but others belong to the races of the elves and dwarfs; as it is said—

"'Methinks the Norns were born far asunder, for they are not of the same race. Some belong to the Æsir, some to the elves, and some are Dvalin's daughters.'

"'But if these Norns dispense the destinies of men,' said Gangler, 'they are, methinks, very unequal in their distribution; for some men are fortunate and wealthy, others acquire neither riches nor honour; some live to a good old age, while others are cut off in their prime.'

"'The Norns,' replied Har, 'Who are of good origin, are good themselves, and dispense good destinies. But those men to whom misfortunes happen ought to ascribe them to the evil Norns.'

"'What more wonders hast thou to tell me,' said Gangler, 'concerning the ash?'

"'What I have further to say respecting it,' replied Har, 'is that there is an eagle perched upon its branches who knows many things; between his eyes sits the hawk called Vedurfölnir. The squirrel named Ratatosk runs up and down the ash, and seeks to cause strife between the eagle and Nidhögg. Four harts run across the branches of the tree and bite the buds. They are called Dáinn, Dvalinn, Duneyr, and Durathrór. But there are so many snakes with Nidhögg in Hvergelmir that no tongue can recount them. As is is said—

'Yggdrasill's ash
More hardship bears
Than men imagine;

> The hart bites above,
> At the sides it rots,
> Below gnaws Nidhögg.'

"And again—
> 'More serpents lie
> Under Yggdrasill's ash
> Than simpletons think of;
> Góinn and Móinn,
> The sons of Grafvitnir,
> Grábak and Gráfyöllud,
> Ofnir and Svafnir,
> Must for aye, methinks,
> Gnaw the roots of that tree.'

"It is also said that the Norns who dwell by the Urdar-fount draw, every day, water from the spring, and with it and the clay that lies around the fount sprinkle the ash, in order that its branches may not rot and wither away. This water is so holy that everything that is placed in the spring becomes as white as the film within an eggshell. As it is said in the Völuspá—

> 'An ash know I standing
> Named Yggdrasill,
> A stately tree sprinkled
> With water the purest
> Hence come the dewdrops
> That fall in the dales;
> Ever blooming, it stands
> O'er the Urdar-fountain.'

"The dew that falls thence on the earth men call honey-dew, and it is the food of the bees. Two fowls are fed in the Urdar-fount; they are called swans, and from them are descended all the birds of this species."

"The Yggdrasill myth, with its three aborescent roots, three fountains, and three destinies, is one of the most significant and poetical to be found in any system of mythology, but its explanation has, as usual, given rise to the most conflicting theories. Grüter and Finn Magnusen offer a physical, Trautwetter an astronomical, Mone an ethical explanation, and Grundtvig applies his favourite theory of the "heoric theory of the north" (Norden's Kæmpe Aand)—pugnacious spirit would be a more appropriate designation—to this, as indeed to every other myth which he treats of, in that most singular and rather too crotchety work of his entitled "Norden's Mythologi."

"According to Finn Magnusen, Yggdrasill is the symbol of universal nature. One of its stems (so he terms the roots) springs from the central primordial abyss—from the subterranean source of matter as it might be termed (Hvergelmir)—runs up through the earth, which it supports, and issuing out of the world's centre, "called Asgard, Caucasus, Borz," &c., spreads its branches over the entire universe. These wide-spreading branches are the ethereal or celestial regions; their leaves, the clouds; their buds or fruits, the stars; the four harts are the four cardinal winds; the eagle is a symbol of the air; the hawk of the wind-still ether; and the squirrel signifies hailstones, snow flakes, vapourous agglomerations, and similar atmospherical phenomona.

"Another stem springs in the warm south over the ethereal Urdar-fountain, the swans swimming in which denote the sun and moon. The third stem takes its rise in the cold and cheerless regions of the north, over the source of the ocean, typified by Mimir's well. The myth of Odin leaving his eye as a pledge to Mimir, signifies the descent of the sun every evening into the sea—to learn wisdom from Mimir during the night; the mead quaffed by Mimir every morning being the ruddy dawn that, spreading over the sky, exhilarates all nature. Nidhögg, and the other monsters that gnaw the fruits of the mundane tree, are the volcanic and other violent torrents that are constantly striving to consume or destroy the earth's foundations.

"Although we agree with Finn Magnusen in regarding Yggdrasill as the symbol of universal nature, we think that in attempting to explain the myth in all its details, he has let his imagination, as usual, get the better of his judgment, and lead him into the most palpable inconsistencies; insomuch so, in fact, that when we begin to examine his theory we are almost tempted to exclaim, with Grundting, "one would think it was meant for a joke." Jacob Grimm —how refreshing it always is to turn to his admirable pages—very justly observes that the whole myth of Yggdrasill bears the stamp of a very high antiquity, but does not appear to be fully unfolded. "We learn," he says, "something respecting the enmity between the eagle and the snake, and that it is kept up by Ratatösk, but nothing as to the destination of the hawk and the four harts."

These remarks of Grimm are fully borne out by the very meagre account given of the Yggdrasill myth in the Völuspá, and the Grimnis-mal, the only Eddaic poems that make mention of it. In order that the reader may be aware on what very slight foundations Finn Magnusen can construct an elaborate theory, we subjoin a literal translation of all the Eddaic strophes that relate to the myth, the words in brackets being inserted to render the obscure passages more intelligible.

"From the Völuspá :—

"St. 17.—'An ash know I standing, called Yggdrasill. A high tree sprinkled with the purest water. Thence comes the dew that falls in the dales. It (the ash) stands evergreen over the Urdar-fountain.'

"18.—'Thence come the much-knowing maidens—three from that lake (fountain) which is under the tree. One is called Urd, another Verdani, and the third Skuld. They engraved (Runic inscriptions, i.e., recorded events) on tablets. They laid down laws; they determined (determine) the life of the sons of men; they tell (fix) the destinies (of men).'

"From Grimnis-mal :—

"St. 29.—'Kormt and Œrmt, and the two Kerlangar—these rivers must Thor wade through every day as he fares to the doomstead under Yggdrasill's ash, otherwise the Æsir-bridge would be in flames, and boiling hot would become the holy waters.'

"30.—'(The horses), Gladr, Gyllir, Glær, Skeidbrimir, Silfirintoppr, Synir, Falhöfnir, Gulltoppr, and Lettfetti, are ridden by the Æsir every day when they go to the doomstead under the ash Yggdrasill.'

"31.—'Three roots stand in three ways (extend to three regions) under the ash Yggdrasill. Hela dwells under one; (under) another (dwell) the Forest-giants; (under) the third (dwell) mortal men' (literally human men).

"32.—'Ratatösk is called the squirrel that shall run (that runs) on the ash Yggdrasill. The eagle's words he shall bear (he bears) downwards, and shall tell (tells) them to Nidhögg below.'

"33.—'There are also four harts that on the summit (of the ash), with bent necks, bite (the leaves), Dain, Dvalin, Duneyr and Durathrór are their names.'

"We think that all that can be gathered from this

account of the ash Yggdrasill, and that given in the Prose Edda, is that the mundane tree is respresented as embracing with its three roots the whole universe; for one of these roots springs from Hvergelmir in Niflheim, another from Mimir's well, situated somewhere or other in the region of the Forest-giants, and the third from the Urdar-fount, which is obviously placed in the celestial regions. We have thus a super-terrestial or supernal (the Urdar) root; a terrestial (the Mimir) root; and a sub-terrestial or infernal (the Hvergelmir) root. That the fountain of the Norns' was supposed to be in the ethereal regions is unquestionable; for we are told in Grimnis-mal that man-kind dwelt under it, and the Prose Edda expressly states that it is "in heaven," and it would appear above Asgard, for the Æsir are described as riding up to the Urdar-fountain. Finn Magnusen, as we have seen, places this fountain and roots issuing from it in the warm south. In his *Eddalæren* he gives us, in fact, to understand that the fountain springs from a high and steep cliff at the south pole, though he admits, for once, that nothing respecting such a cliff is to be found in the Eddaic Poems; the only authority he is able to adduce in support of this strange hypothesis being a figurative expression made use of by a Skald, in a poem written after his conversion to Christianity. Finn Magnusen is also of opinion that the pure water with which the tree is sprinkled by the Norns means "the snow agglomerated in the northern sky," and that "dew that falls in the dales," signifies the ever verdant aspect of the southern parts of the earth, as well as the clear azure sky by which this perennial verdure is canopied.

Mone regards the ash as the emblem of human life. Man is born of water; the swan is therefore the infantile soul that swims on the water: but the eagle, the mature experienced mind that soars aloft; the hawk perched between the eagle's eyes being eternal sensation. The snakes that gnaw the root of life are the vices and passions; the squirrel, the double-tongued flatterer, constantly running between these passions and the mind (the eagle) which has raised itself above their control. The harts denote the passions of the mind, folly, madness, terror and disquietude, and therefore feed on the healthy thoughts (the green leaves). But as man in his levity remarks not what enemies threaten his existence, the stem rots on the side, and many a one dies before he attains to wisdom, or figuratively before the bird of his soul (the eagle) is seated amidst the perennial verdure of the mundane tree.

Ling supposes Yggdrasill to be the symbol both of universal and human life, and its three roots to signify the physical, the intellectual, and the moral principles.

Other writers cited by Finn Magnusen take these roots to have been meant for matter, organization and spirit, and the ash itself for the symbol of universal primordial vitality."

The translator of Mallet adds in a note: "The ash was the most appropriate tree that could have been chosen for such an emblem. Virgil describes it with its outspreading branches as enduring for centuries, and it is a singular coincidence that he should have represented it as a tree that reaches with its roots as far downwards as it does upwards with its branches. We may here remark that the maypole and the German *Christbaum* have a Pagan origin, the type of both being the ash Yggdrasill."

Strahlenberg informs us that the Czeremisi or Scheremissi were a Pagan people under the government of Casan. Those who lived on the right side of the Wolga were called Sanagornya, and those on the left side of that river Lugowija. These people had no idols of wood or stone, but directed their prayers to heaven in the open air, and near great trees to which they paid honour, holding their assemblies about them. The hides and bones of the cattle they sacrificed they hung about these holy trees to rot, by way of sacrifice to the air.

The Jakuhti were a Pagan people under the Russian Government, along the river Lena and about the city of Jakutskoi.

While not actually worshipping idols carved in wood, like the Ostiaks and Tungusü, they had a type or image of their invisible god stuffed out with a body like a bag, with monstrous head and eyes of coral. This image they hung upon a tree and round it the furs of sables and other animals. They had many superstitious customs in common with other nations, which they celebrated about certain trees

* Percy's "Mallet's Northern Antiquities."

regarded as sacred. When they met with a fine tree they hung all manner of nick-nacks about it—of iron, brass copper, &c. They are said to have carried nine different sorts of things for offerings to their Hayns or idolatrous groves.

Their priests, when they performed their rites, put on garments trimmed with bits of iron, rattles and bells. As soon as the fields began to be green, each generation gathered together at a place where there was a fine tree and a pleasant spot of ground. There they sacrificed horses and oxen, the heads of which they stuck up round the trees.

Strahlenberg, speaking of the Pagans in Russia (of 150 years ago), says: "In general it may be said of them all, that they believe one Eternal Being, who created all things, and whom they pretend to worship under the form of many sorts of strange things. Some of them have taken a fancy to many sorts of images; some to animals, birds, and stars; they set apart for their offerings, which they make to heaven, certain places or holy groves, and have regard to fire and other elements."*

In the interesting dictionary of Mr. Peter Bayle, under Rubenus (Leonard), we have a notice of Tree Worship which may very well be introduced here as assisting generally with our discussion of the subject.

Rubenus was a native of Essen in Germany, and entered the order of St. Benedict at Cologne in the year 1596. He was in Transylvania in the year 1588, and he there published theses concerning idolatry, dedicating them to Prince Sigismund Battori. He relates a thing which shews that Livonia was still infected with heathenish idolatry. Having received an order from his superiors to go to Dorpat, which is almost the outmost town of Livonia, in his way he passed through the sacred woods of the Esthonians. He saw there a pine tree of an extraordinary height and size, the branches whereof were full of divers pieces of old cloth, and its roots covered with many bundles of straw and hay. He asked a man of the neighbourhood what was the meaning of it; he answered that the inhabitants adored that tree, and that the women after a safe delivery brought thither these bundles of hay; that they also had a custom to offer at a certain time a tun

* Descrip. N. and E. of Europe, p. 289.

of beer, and to throw a tun of it into the lake of Mariemburg when it thundered, and that they thought the thunder was the son of God, and that he was appeased by the effusion of that liquor. He desired they would bring him a good hatchet, for that which he had in his chariot was not sharp; and when they asked him what he designed to do with it, I will show you, said he, the weakness of what you worship. The Esthonians replied that they could not do what he desired without the utmost danger, and cried to him to take care of going under the tree, and if he did both he and his chariot would be taken up into the air. However, he made his horses go under it; and, taking his hatchet, in a devout manner he cut the figure of a cross on the pine, and lest that figure made by a man, whom they honoured with the appellation of the great temple of God, should increase their superstition, he cut a gibbet on the same tree, and, in derision, said—behold your God.

"There is no mistake," says a writer in Fraser (1871), "as to our old Tree and Serpent faiths. Each hamlet (he is speaking of his visit to Ammer in Bavaria) has its Maienbaum—a long pole, one hundred feet or more in height, with alternate blue and white stripes coiling round it. The May-pole is intersected by seven or sometimes nine bars, beginning at about ten feet from the ground and running to the top, which is adorned with streamers. On these bars are various emblematic figures. The one at Murau had on the lower limb a small tree and a nail with circular nob; on the next a small house, a horseshoe and wheel on one side; a hammer crossed by a pair of pincers on the other, a broom, perhaps Ceres as a sheaf of corn; below this was seen the Lingam, with Maya's symbols, the cup and cock or the bird of desire sacred to her. Elsewhere we see a heart, fire, pyramid, and inverted pyramid, anchor and water as in Egypt, and a circle pierced by a line, &c. Can any Phallic tale be more complete? We must be here content with our general knowledge that the Maienbaum was a Pagan object, and that its decorations were originally symbols of the gods and goddesses. Christian significance is given to all these; for as the priest could not efface the old faiths he told his credulous herd that this hammer is that which nailed

Christ to the cross, that the tree is the conventional olive of church pictures, and that the cross, the cock, the cup and sacred heart are all connected with the "Passion of Christ." The broom represents witches, and the horseshoe the corona or Mary's head dress; it is also Maiya's sign, and is there as a charm to hold witches at bay like the Ephod of old. He who may, I fancy, be taken as one great tree of life.

"On May-day it is festooned with branches, for the Bavarian peasants keep up, in many ways, the ancient reverence for sacred trees.

"When a house is finished it is consecrated by having a birch sapling stuck into the roof, and in a thousand tales the poor and ignorant are still taught to fear trees. One story says that before a large fir tree King Ludwig's horse fell three times forward on his knees, and here he built a celebrated church, taking care that the fir tree should be in its very centre."

"The most interesting feature of the Passion Play to me," continues the writer, "was that nine young birch trees, reaching from floor to ceiling, had been set along the walls inside, at intervals of ten to fifteen feet. That the sacred tree of ancient Germany and even of ancient Greece, which has so long been held as a charm against witches, against lightning and other evils, should be here overshadowing Christian worshippers was curious enough. The enclosure was also surrounded by birch trees, regularly planted. Like our remote ancestors who worshipped Odin, we sat amidst the sacred grove. There are some remote corners of these mountains, it is said, where one who has a fever still goes to a birch tree and shakes it, with the words: 'Birch, a fever plagues me; God grant it may pass from me to thee!' and where one subject to cramp takes a broom made of birch switches into his bed. The presence of these trees is one among the features of the Ammergau Play which justify antiquaries in tracing its origin to a period far anterior to that with which it is connected in the records of the village. The story has often been told of how, nearly two and a half centuries ago, a pilgrim came to some sacred festival in the village and brought with him a plague which devastated it; how the people got together and united in a holy vow, that if their village were spared further ravages they would, every tenth year, represent solemnly the sufferings and death of Christ; and how immediately the scourge was removed, not another person dying even of those who lay sick when the vow was made. But though the villagers do not care to look beyond this story on their records, the legend itself suggests that there was already some festival there which had attracted the pilgrim who brought them so much woe. Professor von Löher informed me that there is some evidence, not only that somewhat similar dramatic performances occurred occasionally at Oberammergau before the period mentioned in the village tradition, but that even far away in Pagan times it was one of the spots where the people represented the deeds of their gods and heroes theatrically. It is well known that in many regions the early Christians avoided all interference with such Pagan customs when they found them preferring to substitute their own sacred characters for those of heathenism. There are probabilities, therefore, that the sacred birches which now surround the scenes of Christian story once witnessed the life and death of Baldur; or that later still, the birch boughs which the children now strew in the path of Christ as he enters Jerusalem, were once cast before the chariot of the Sun-god, to symbolize the fresh foliage with which his warm beams invested the earth."

The same writer adds: "With the birch trees waving around, and these old symbols of once great religions before me, I felt thrilled by an impression of having reached a spot where the prehistoric religion could be traced visibly blending with Christianity."

Tree and Serpent worship is the theme of many an ancient Greek myth. The destruction of the dragon Python by Apollo, who takes possession of the oracle which the serpent guarded; the conversion of Cadmus and his wife into serpents when they were regarded as objects of veneration; the story of the Argonautic expedition, which was undertaken to recover a fleece that hung on a tree guarded by a dragon; the strangling of serpents by Hercules; his adventure in the garden of the Hesperides, which reminds us of the garden of Eden, though with a different moral; his fight with Lernaean hydra; on the other hand, his intercourse with the serpent Echidna, through whom he is said to have become the progenitor of the whole race of serpent-worshipping Scythians; the keeping of serpents at Delphi and other places for oracular purposes; the serpent worship at Epidaurus, where stood the temple of Æsculapius and the grove attached to it; the contention between Athene and Poseidon for the guardianship of the city of Athens when the goddess created the olive, planting it on the Acropolis, and handed over the care of it to the serpent-god Ericthonius; the statement that when the Persians were approaching Athens the Athenians, though warned by the oracle, refused to leave their homes till they learned that the great serpent, the guardian of the city, had refused its food and left its place; the curious record concerning the descent of Alexander the Great from a serpent; the part which snakes played in the Bacchic cultus—all these tales show the tenacity of that early form of worship.

Fergusson adds to this summary of his words by an American writer:—"The traces of Tree Worship in Greece are even fuller and more defined than those of the Serpent Cultus just alluded to. As each succeeding Buddha in the Indian mythology had a separate and different Bo-tree assigned to him, so each god of the classical Pantheon seems to have had some tree appropriated as his emblem or representative. Among the most familiar are the oak or beech of Jupiter, the laurel of Apollo, the vine of Bacchus. The olive is the well-known tree of Minerva. The myrtle was sacred to Aphrodite. The apple or orange of the Hesperides belonged to Juno. The populus was the tree of Hercules, and the plane-tree was the "numen of Atridæ."

We have now presented a view of this interesting cultus extending over the principal nations of the Eastern and Western worlds, and reaching from the remotest ages to modern times. In doing so, many curious legends and superstitious customs have been described upon the best authority, and, in most instances, upon the testimony of actual eye witnesses. The story must now stop as our usual limits have been reached; it will probably be resumed again in a future volume, which it is hoped will, in conjunction with its predecessors, form a complete exposition of the mysteries of what is called Phallic Worship.

Bibliography of Authorities consulted and referred to in the preparation of these volumes.

CLASS I.

SPECIAL WORKS UPON THE PHALLIC CULTUS.

BOUDIN (J. C.) Etudes Anthropologiques, Considerations sur le Culte et les pratiques réligieuses de divers peuples anciens et modernes; Culte du Phallus; Culte du Serpent; 8vo, pp. 88   *Paris*, 1864

CAMPBELL (R. A.) Phallic Worship, an Outline of the Worship of the Generative Organs, as being or as representing the Divine Creator, with Suggestions as to the influence of the Phallic idea on religious Creeds, Ceremonies, Customs, and Symbolism, past and present; 200 illustrations   *St. Louis, U.S.A.*, 1887

DAVENPORT (J.) Aphrodisiacs and Anti-Aphrodisiacs, three essays on the Phallic Worship and Powers of Reproduction; illustrated, 4to
    Privately printed, 1869

DAVENPORT (J.) Curiositates Eroticæ Physiologie, or a Tabooed Subject freely treated; 4to   *Privately Printed*, 1869

DULAURE (J. A.) Des Divinités Génératrices, ou du Culte du Phallus chez les anciens et les modernes; 1st edition, 8vo, pp. xxiv. 428   *Paris*, 1805

DULAURE (J. A.) Histoire abregée de differens Cultes, des Cultes qui ont précédé et améné l'idolatrie ou l'adoration des figures humains (vol. 1); et des Divinités génératrices chez les anciens et les modernes (vol. 2); 2 vols 8vo, pp. x. 558, xvi. 464   *Paris*, 1825

[The 2nd vol. is a reprint of foregoing considerably enlarged, and was *suppressed*.]

DULAURE (J. A.) Des Divinités Génératrices, ou de Culte du Phallus, chez les anciens et les modernes, augmentée par l'auteur; 8vo, pp. xvi. 422   *Paris (Siseux)*, 1885

[A reprint of the suppressed 2nd vol. of the 1825 edition]

DOMENECH (l'Abbé) Manuscrit pictographique Américain, précédé d'une notice sur l'idéographie des Peux—Rouges; 8vo, 228 pp. of illustrations
Paris, 1860

DOMENECH (l'Abbé) La Verité sur le "Livre des Savages;" 10 pp. of plates and text, 8vo
Paris, 1861

FORLONG (Major-General) Rivers of Life, or Sources and Streams of the Faiths of Man in all Lands, with maps, many illustrations, and large coloured chart of Faith Streams; 2 vols. 4to, pp. xii. 565 and 659, and chart in case
London, 1883

D'HANCARVILLE (P. F. Hugues) Monumens de la vie privée des douze Césars, d'après une suite de pierres gravées sans leur regne; 4to, front. and 50 plates and text
à Rome, 1786

D'HANCARVILLE (P. F. Hugues) Monumens du Culte Secret des Dames Romaines, d'après, &c., &c., pour Servir de Suite à la vie des douze Césars; 4to, front. and 50 plates and text
à Rome, 1790
[Both works since reprinted.]

INMAN (Thos., M.D.) Ancient Faiths embodied in Ancient Names, an attempt to trace the religious belief, sacred rites, and holy emblems of certain nations, by an interpretation of the names given to childhood, &c.; 3 vols. 8vo, privately printed
London, 1869

[The 3rd vol. having the same title was printed, but not published, and in that form is excessively rare; but it was subsequently reprinted with a different title and other alterations, as:

"Ancient Faiths and Modern, a Dissertation upon Worships, Legends and Divinities, in Central and and Eastern Asia, Europe and elsewhere, before the Christian era, showing their relations to religious customs as they now exist; 8vo
New York, 1876"]

INMAN (Thos., M.D.) Ancient, Pagan and Modern Christian Symbolism, 2 edition, enlarged with Essay on Baal-Worship, the Assyrian G. yes, and other allied symbols, by John Newton, M.R.C.S.; 8vo, many illustrations
London, 1875

JENNINGS (Hargrave) Phallism, celestial and terrestrial, heathen and Christian, its connexion with the Rosicrucians and the Gnostics, and its foundation in Buddhism, with an Essay on Mystic Anatomy; 8vo, pp. xxvii. 298
London, 1884

JENNINGS (Hargrave) Illustrations of Phallism, consisting of ten plates of remains of ancient Art, with descriptions; 8vo
London, 1885

KNIGHT (R. P.) An Account of the Remains of the Worship of Priapus, lately existing at Isernia, in the Kingdom of Naples, in two Letters, one from Sir William Hamilton, K.B. ... to Sir Joseph Banks ... and the other from a person residing at Isernia; to which is added A Discussion on the Worship of Priapus, and its connexion with the mystic Theology of the Ancients; 4to, pp. 195, 18 plates and an extra one
London, 1786

KNIGHT (R. P.) A Discourse on the Worship of the Priapus, and its connexion with the mystic theology of the Ancients; to which is added, An Essay on the Worship of the Generative Powers during the middle ages of Western Europe; 4to, pp. xvi. 254, and 40 plates, p.p.
London, 1865
[The "Essay" is understood to have been written by the late Thos. Wright, assisted by Sir James Emerson Tennent and Mr. George Witt; 125 copies were printed, of which six were on large paper, and are naturally very scarce.]

KNIGHT (R. P.) Le Culte de Priape et les rapports avec la Théologie Mystique des Anciens, par Richard Payne Knight, Suivi d'un Essai sur le Culte des Pouvoirs générateurs durant le moyen age, traduits de l'Anglais, par E.W. (said to have been Madame Yga); 4to, pp. viii. 224, 40 plates, Luxembourg *Brussels*, 1886
[110 copies only printed.]

KNIGHT (R. P.) Do.   do.,   4to, pp. xviii. 200, 40 plates
[500 copies printed.] *Bruxelles*, 1883

KNIGHT (R. P.) The Worship of Priapus, an Account of the Fête of St. Cosmo and Damiano, celebrated at Isernia in 1780, in a letter to Sir Joseph Banks . . . . In which is added, Some Account of the Phallic Worship, principally derived from a Discourse on the Worship of Priapus, by Richard Payne Knight, edited by Hargrave Jennings . .; 4to, pp. xi. 37 *London*, 1883
[100 copies printed.]

MACFIE (M.) Religious Parallelisms, and Symbolisms ancient and modern (Phallic Worship, &c.); 8vo *London*, 1879

MULJI (Karsandás) History of the Sect of Mahárájas, or Vallabácháryas in Western India; 8vo, pp. xv. 182 and app. 183, illustrated
London, 1865
[500 copies were printed, but only 75 reserved for sale in Europe, the rest were sent to Bombay, so the work is now scarce.]

O'BRIEN (Henry) The Round Towers of Ireland, or the History of the Tuath de Danaans for the first time unveiled; 8vo, illustrated
London, 1834
[A "curious" Preface is to be found in the earlier impressions.]

OPHIOLATREIA.—An Account of the Rites and Mysteries connected with the Origin, Rise and Development of Serpent Worship, Serpent Mounds and Temples, the whole forming an exposition of one of the phases of Phallic or Sex Worship; 8vo, vellum p.p., *London*, 1889

PHALLISM.—A Description of the Worship of Lingam-Yoni in various parts of the World and in different Ages, with an Account of ancient and modern Crosses, particularly of the Crux Ansata, and other Symbols connected with the Mysteries of Sex Worship; 8vo
p.p., *London*, 1889

PHALLIC WORSHIP.—A Description of the Mysteries of the Sex Worship of the Ancients, with the History of the Masculine Cross; 8vo
p.p., *London*, 1886

PHALLIC OBJECTS, Monuments and Remains, Illustrations of the Rise and Development of the Phallic Idea (Sex Worship) and its embodiment in Works of Nature and Art; 8vo, etched frontispiece
p.p., *London*, 1889

PHALLIC OBJECTS AND REMAINS.—Catalogo del Museo Nazionale di Napoli, Raccolta Pornographica (Phallic Collection); folio
Napoli, 1866

PHALLIC OBJECTS AND REMAINS.—Guide pour la Musée Royal Bourbon, par Verde, trad. par C. C. J. (Phallic Collection, 161 subjects, ii. pp. 169-194); 2 vols. 8vo
Naples, 1831-2

PHALLIC OBJECTS AND REMAINS.—Musée Royal de Naples, Peintures, Bronzes, et Statues érotiques du Cabinet Sécret, avec notes explicatives de plusieurs auteurs; 62 gravs. coloriées, 2 vols. 4to
Bruxelles, 1876

PHALLIC OBJECTS AND REMAINS.—The Secret Museum of Naples, being an account of the Erotic Paintings, Bronzes and Statues contained in that famous "Cabinet Secret," by Col. Fanin; 4to, 60 full-page illustrations, some coloured
p.p., *London*, 1872

PHALLIC OBJECTS AND REMAINS.—Histoire des Antiquités de la villo de Nismes et de ses Environs, extrait de M. Ménard, 1st edition, 1829, avec Supplément et de Notes, &c. (with curious plates of Phallic Remains); 8vo
Nimes, 1829-30

Do. do. 5th edition, par Perrot; 8vo, enlarged
Nismes, 1834

PHALLIC OBJECTS AND REMAINS.—Herculaneum et Pompéi, Recueil général des Peintures, Bronzes, Mosaïques .... augmenté de sujets inédits, gravés au trait sur cuivre, par H. Roux ainé, et accompagné d'un texto explicatif par M. L. Barré; 8 vols. 8vo
Paris, 1875-6

[The Phallic collection—la Musée Secret—is in a separate case.]

[ROCCO (Sha)] The Masculine Cross and Ancient Sex Worship; *woodcut illustrations*, crown 8vo
New York, 1874

ROLLE (P.N.) Recherches sur le Culte de Bacchus, symbole de la force reproductive de la Nature, sous ses rapports généraux dans les mystères d'Eleusis, les Dionysiaques; 3 vols. 8vo
Paris, 1824

ROSENBAUM (Dr. J.) Geschichte der Lustseuche im Alterthume, nebst ausführlichen untersuchungen über den Venus, und Phallus Cultus, Bordelle, Paederastie, &c. ....; 2nd edition, pp. 464, 8vo *Halle*, 1845

Do. do. 3rd edition, pp. 484, 8vo
Halle, 1882

Do. traduct. Française par Santluz, in Archives de la Medicine Belge; 3 vols. 8vo
1845-6-7

SELLON (E.) Annotations on the Sacred Writings of the Hindûs, being an Epitome of some of the most remarkable and leading tenets in the faiths of that people; 8vo
p.p., *London*, 1865

SELLON (E.) On the Phallic Worship of India (in Mems. Anthrop. Socy., i. pp. 327-334)
London, 1865

SELLON (E.) On Indian Gnosticism, or Sacti Puja, the Worship of the Female Powers, pp. 12 (in Mems. Anthrop. Socy., ii. 264-276)
London, 1866

SIMPSON (H. T.) Archaeologia Adelensis, a History of the Parish of Adel (Yorks); 8vo *London*, 1879

[Phallic Worship is treated fully pp. 154-158, with many etchings of Phallic Rockmarkings, by W. L. Ferguson.]

VENERES ET PRIAPI, ut observantur in gemmis antiquis; 8vo, 70 plates *Lugdun Batov.*

[In several editions—an English one quite recently.]

WAKE (C. Staniland) Serpent Worship and other Essays, Phallism in Ancient Religions, Sacred Prostitution, &c., with a chapter on Totemism; 8vo *London*, 1888

WAKE (C. Staniland) Ancient Symbol Worship, Influence of the Phallic Idea in the Religions of Antiquity, by H. Westropp and Staniland Wake, with Introduction and Notes by Dr. Wilder; 2nd edition, illustrated, 8vo *New York*, 1875

WESTROPP (II. M.) Primitive Symbolism, as illustrated in Phallic Worship or the Reproductive Principle, with Introduction by General Forlong; 8vo *London*, 1885

PRIAPEIA, or the Sportive Epigrams of divers Poets on Priapus, now first completely done into English prose from the original Latin, with Introduction, Notes explanatory and illustrative, an excursûs, to which is appended the Latin text; 8vo p.p., *London*, 1889

CLASS II.

Works Referring Incidentally to the Phallic Cultus
and closely allied subjects.

Abbe de Tressau's Heathen Mythology
Acosta's History of the Indies
Æschylus
Alabaster's Modern Buddhist
All the Year Round, vol. vii.
Ancient Pillar Stones of Scotland, Aberdeen, 1865
Anderson's Constitutions
Anthropological Society's Transactions [The Memoirs]
Antiquities of Orissa Rajendralala Mitra
Archæologia Scotia
Aristophanes
Arundale's Jerusalem and Sinai
Asiatic Researches
Bacchic Mysteries, On the—Pamphleteer, vol. viii.
Bardwell's Temples
Banier's Mythology, iv. vols.,

BIBLIOGRAPHY.

Baring Gould's Myths of Middle Ages
Baring Gould's Origin and Development of Religious Belief
Barker's Ancient World
  „   Aryan Civilization
Barlow on Symbolism
Bastian's Beginnings of Life
Barth's Religions of India
Bateman's Ten Years' Diggings
Bayle's Dictionary
Beale's Legends of Buddha
Bede's Ecclesiastical History
Bellamy's History of Religions
Bernier's Travels in Mogul Empire
Betham's Etruria Celtica
Bird's Travel's in Japan
Birdwood's Indian Arts
Blair's Chronology
Blavatsky's Isis unveiled
Bonwick's Egyptian Beliefs
Borlase's Antiquities of Cornwall
Bradford's American Antiquities
Brand's Popular Antiquities, iii. vols.
Bruite's Myths of the New World
British Quarterly, 34
Brown's Vulgar Errors
Bryant's Analysis
Buchanan's Journey from Madras, iii. vols.
  „   Researches in Asia
Buckingham's Travels in Palestine, ii. vols.
Bullock's Mexican Exhibition
Burckhardt's Travels in Nubia, &c.
Burden's Oriental Customs
Burton's Travels
Calcutta Review
Callcott on Freemasonry
Calmet's Antiquities
  „   Dictionary
Camden's Britannia by Gough, iv. vols.
Carne's Letters from the East
Catholic World, vi., ix.
Chambers's Journal, viii., xix., xxii.
Chardin's Travels in Persia, ii. vols.
Clarke's Prehist. Compar. Philology
Clarke's Travels in Greece and Albania
  „   Travels, vi. vols.
Classical Magazine
Closmadeuc, G.—Sculptures Lapidaires et Signes Graves des dolmens dans le Morbihan; many plates, 8vo. Vannes, 1873.
Colbourn's Mythology, v.
Coleman's Mythology of the Hindus
Collyer (R.), Ilkley, Ancient and Modern

BIBLIOGRAPHY 105

Comical Pilgrim's Pilgrimage to Ireland
Contemporary Review, xii.
Conway's Sacred Anthology
Cooper's Archaic Dictionary
Cornhill Magazine, xix.
Cory's Ancient Fragments
Cox's Aryan Mythology.
Crawfurd's History of the Indian Archipelago
Cudworth's Intellectual System
Cunningham's Ancient Geography of India
Davies on British Coins
D'Anville on Ancient Geography
Davies's Celtic Researches
„ History and Mythology of the Druids
„ Unorthordox London
Dawkins's Early Man
Dean's Worship of the Serpent
Delaure's Culte du Phallus
Denon's Travels in Egypt
Didron's Christian Iconography
Dinsdall's Isocrates
Diodorus
Dow's History of Hindostan
Dowson's Dictionary of Hindu Mythology
Dublin Penny Journal, viii. vols
Dublin University Magazine
Dubois on the Institutions of India
Du Halde's History of China
Duncker's History of Antiquities
Dupuis's Origine de tout les Cultes
Eclectic Magazine, lxxii.
Edinburgh Magazine
Eleusinian Mysteries, On the—Pamphleteer, vol. viii.
Englishwoman in Russia
Euripides
Eusebius
Faber's Mysteries of the Cabirri
„ Pagan Idolatry
Farrer's Primitive Customs
Fellows's Mysteries of Freemasonry
Fenton's History of Pembrokeshire
Furgusson's Rock Cut Temples of India
„ Rude Stone Monuments
„ Tree and Serpent Worship
Fleury's Manners of the Ancient Israelites
Forbin's Travels in the Holy Land
Forester's Sardinia
Foquet (A.) Guide des Jouristes et des Archeologues dans le Morbihan : nouv. ed., 12mo. 1873.
Fraser's Magazine, lxxxii.
Gage's Survey of the West Indies

BIBLIOGRAPHY.

Gale's Court of the Gentiles, iii. vols., 4to.
Gibbon's Roman Empire
Gill's Myths of the South Pacific
Glass's History of the Canary Isles
Glennie's Pilgrim Memories
Good Words, xiii., xiv.
Goranson's Histories in Mallet's Northern Antiquities
Gorins's Etruscan Antiquities
Gray's Sculptures of Etruria
Grimm's Tuetonic Mythology
Grose's Antiquities of England, Scotland and Ireland
Grose's Provincial Glossary
   ,,   Voyage to the East Indies
Grote's History of Greece
Gumpach's History of Antiquities of Egypt
Haeckel's History of Creation
Hales's Analysis of Chronology
Halhed's Code of Gentoo Law
Hamilton's Egyptica
Hanway's Persia
Harper's Magazine, xli.
Haslam's Cross and Serpent Worship
Heeren's Ancient History
Herbert's Antiquity of Stonehenge
Herodotus
Hesiod
Heywood's Cup and Ring Stones of Ilkley, Yorkshire
Hibbert Lectures for 1878 and 1880
Higgins's Anacalypsis
   ,,   Druids
Holwell on the Feasts of the Hindoos
Holwell's Historical Events
   ,,   Mythological Dictionary
Hone's Ancient Mysteries
Horus and Serpent Myths—Cooper Vic. Inst.
Hours at Home, i.
Household Words, xv., xvi.
Huc's Travel's in Thibet, &c.
Humboldt's Monuments of Ancient Inhabitants of America
   ,,   Personal Narrative, vii.
Hunter's Imperial Gazetteer of India
   ,,   Non-Aryan Languages
   ,,   Rural Bengal
Hutchinson's History of Cumberland
   ,,   Spirit of Masonry
   ,,   Two Years in Peru
Indian Antiquary
International Magazine
Irving's Bracebridge Hall
Jamieson's Scottish Dictionary
Jenning's Jewish Antiquities

Jenning's Rosicrucians
Jones's (Sir W.) Works
Jones's (Stephen) Masonic Miscellanies
Josephus
Journal of Asiatic Society of Bengal
   ,,   Forestry, vol. viii.
Joyce's History of Irish Names
   ,, Old Celtic Romances
Kœmpfers' History of Japan
Kerney's Outlines of Primitive Belief
Keane's Towers and Temples of Ireland
Keightly's Mythology
Kelly's Indu-European Traditions
Kennett's Roman Antiquities
Kenrick's Ancient Egypt
   ,,   Phœnicia
Kilkenny Archæological Journal
Kitto's Journal of Sacred Literature
Klaproth's Travels in the Caucasus
Knight's (Payne) Symbolic Language
Lamb's Hieroglyphics
Landseer's Sabœan Researches
Latham's Ethnology of the British Isles.
Laurie's Freemasonry in Scotland
Laws of Manu
Layard's Nineveh and Babylon
Le Compte's Memoirs of China
Ledwich's Antiquities of Ireland
Leslie's Ancient Races of Scotland
   ,, Ceylon
   ,, Origin of Man
Lewis's Origines Hebrœcœ
Lord's Banian Religion
Lubbock's Pre-historic times
   ,,   Origin of Civilization
Lucan's Pharsalia
Lucretius's Nature of Things
Lundy's Monumental Christianity
Lyell's Asiatic Studies
Maclagan's Scottish Myths
Maclean's Celtic Language
Macpherson's Indian Khonds
Madden's Shrines and Sepulchres
Maimonides de Idolatria
Mailland's Church of the Catacombs
Malcolm's History of Persia
   ,,   Memoirs of Central India
Mallet's Northern Antiquities
Manning's Ancient and Mediæval India
Macquoid's journey through Brittany
Marco Polo's Travels by Yule

Marshman's History of India
Massey's Book of Beginnings
Maundrell's Journey
Maurice's Ancient History of Hindostan
   ,,   Indian Antiquities, vii. vols.
   ,,   Modern History of Hindostan
Meyrick's History of Cardigan
Mill's History of Chivalry
Mill's History of the Crusades
Milman's History of the Jews
Montfaucon, L'Antiquité expliquée
Moore's Ancient Stones of Scotland
Moor's Hindu Pantheon
Morris's New Nation
Moule's Fish Heraldry
Mounier's Influence of Freemasonry on the French Revolution
Muir's Mahomet and Hist. of Islam
Nature, xvii.
Newton's Chronology
Niebuhr's Voyage in Arabia
Nieuhoff's Travels in India
Nightingale's Religious Ceremonies of all nations
Nineteenth Century, iv., vii.
Norden's Travels in Egypt and Nubia
North American Review, cx.
O'Brien's Round Towers of Ireland
Ockley's Saracens
Old Statistical Account of Scotland
Oliphant's Land of Gilead
Oliver (L. P.), Megalithic Structures of the Channel Islands, their History and Analogies, 1870
Oliver's Antiquities of Masonry
   ,,   History of Beverley
   ,,   History of Initiation into Ancient Rites
   ,,   Signs and Symbols
   ,,   Star in the East
O'Neill's Fine Arts of Ancient Ireland
Oort's Worship of Baalim
Orme's Historical Fragments
   ,,   Transactions in India
Osburn's Monumental Egypt
Ousley's Travels in the East
Ovid
Owen's Serpent Worship
Palgrave's Arabia
Palmyra, Antiquities of
Pampheteer, The
Parsons's Remains of Japheth
Pausanias
Pennant's Fire Worship in India
   ,,   Journey to Alston Moor

Pennant's Tour in Scotland
Petrie's Round Towers of Ireland
Philpot's Heraldry
Picart's Religious Ceremonies
Pindar's Odes
Pinkerton's Collection of Travels
Pliny's Natural History
Plutarch's Lives
Pococke's India in Greece
Pontoppidon's History of Norway
Popular Science Review, xvii.
Potter's Archæology
    ,,   Grecian Antiquities
Prescott's Conquest of Mexico
    ,,   Conquest of Peru
Preston's Illustrations of Masonry
Prideaux's Connection
Pritchard's Celtic Nations
Propertius
Purchas's Pilgrim
    ,,   Voyages and Travels
Quarterly Review, cxiv.
Raleigh's History of the World
Ramsay on the Theology of the Pagans
Reade's Veil of Isis
Renouf's Hibbert Lectures
Rivett, Carnac, Snake Myths of India
Roberts's Cambrian Antiquities
Robertson's History of America
Rolle's Recherches sur le Culte de Bacchus
Rollins's Ancient History
Ross's View of all Religions
Rou (C.) Cup-shaped and other Sculptures in the Old World and in America, 1881
Rousselet's India and its Princes
Royal Institutions of Cornwall
Royal Irish Academy, Transactions
Rust's Druidism Exhumed
Sacred Books of the East, many vols.
Sale's Koran
Sanhita of Sama Veda—Thomson's Translation
Samme's Britannia
Satires of Persæus
Savary's Letters on Egypt
    ,,   Letters on Greece
Sayce's Lectures
Schlieman's Mycenæ and Tiryns
Secret Societies of the Middle Ages
Seeley's Wonders of Elora
Seldon's Fabulous God's Denounced in the Bible
Septchenes's Religion of the Ancient Greeks

Sharpe's Hebrew Nation
Simpson's Archæological Essays
Simpson (Sir J.) Archaic Sculpturings of Cups, &c., upon Stones and Rocks in Scotland, England and other countries.
Sinclair's Statist, vol. xvii.
Skene's Celtic Scotland
Skertchly's Dahomy as it is
Smiddy's Druids and Towers of Ireland
Smith's Chaldean Genesis
  ,, Greek and Roman Antiquities
Society of Antiquaries of Scotland, Proceedings
Sonnerat's Voyages
Socrates Eccles. Hist.
Spencer's Ceremonial Institutions
Spineto's Lectures
Squier's Serpent Symbols
St. James's Magazine, xxv.
Stanley's Eastern Races
  ,, History of the Philosophers
  ,, Sinai and Palestine
Stephens's Yucatan and Central America
Strabo's Geography
Strahlenberg's Description of N. and E. Europe and Asia
Strange's Developement of Creation
Stukeley's Itinerary
  ,, Stonehenge and Abury
Tavernier's Voyages
Taylor's Etruscan Researches
  ,, Hymns of Orpheus
  ,, Mexico and the Mexicans
  ,, Proclus
Tenison's Idolatry
Thales's Origin of Mankind
The Living Age, xx., cxxxix.
Thevènot's Travels into the Levant
Tiele's History of Ancient Religions
Tod's Antiquities of Rajasthan
Toland's History of the Druids
Tooke's Pantheon
Transactions of the Royal Society of Literature
Turnbull's Voyage Round the World
Turner's History of the Anglo-Saxons
Tylor's Primitive Culture
Ulster Journal of Archæology
Unitarian Review, Boston
Universe Displayed, iv. vols.
Upham's Buddhism
Urquhart's Spirit of the East
Vallancey's Ancient Irish Language
  ,, Bulgaria
  ,, Colec. de Rebus Hibern

Vancouvre's Voyage Round the World
Virgil's Works
Volney's Travels in Syria
Wait's Jewish Antiquities
  ,, Oriental Antiquities
Wakeman's Archæologia Hibernica
Ward's View of the Hindoos
Waring's Monuments and Ornament
Wheeler's History of India
Weber's Indian Literature
Welsh Archæology
Westropp's Archæological Handbook
Wilder's Ancient Symbol Worship
Wilkinson's Ancient Egypt
Willis's Current Notes
Wilson's Egypt of the Past
  ,, Pre-historic Annals of Scotland
Wormius's Danish Monuments
Young's Egyptian Antiquities
Xenophon Anabasis

PHALLIC SERIES

Cr. 8vo, Vellum, 7/6 Each.

Only a *very limited number*, privately printed.

PHALLICISM.—A Description of the Worship of **Lingam-Yoni** in various parts of the World, and in different Ages, with an Account of Ancient and Modern Crosses, particularly of the **Crux Ansata** (or Handled Cross) and other Symbols connected with the Mysteries of **Sex Worship.**
Nearly out of print.

OPHIOLATREIA.—An Account of the Rites and Mysteries connected with the Origin, Rise, and Development of **Serpent Worship** in various parts of the World, enriched with Interesting Traditions, and a full description of the celebrated Serpent Mounds and Temples, the whole forming an exposition of one of the phases of **Phallic, or Sex Worship.**

PHALLIC OBJECTS, Monuments and Remains; Illustrations of the Rise and Development of the **Phallic Idea** (Sex Worship), and its embodiment in Works of Nature and Art. *Etched Frontispiece.*

CULTUS ARBORUM.—A Descriptive Account of **Phallic Tree Worship,** with illustrative Legends, Superstitious Usages, &c.; exhibiting its Origin and Development amongst the Eastern and Western Nations of the World, from the earliest to modern times.

IN PREPARATION.

FISHES, FLOWERS, AND FIRE as Phallic Symbols.

www.ingramcontent.com/pod-product-compliance
Lightning Source LLC
Chambersburg PA
CBHW020135170426
43199CB00010B/759